Praise for *Kate Chopin*

*A fresh and personal look at the material con_____ k,
exploring how local spaces and global issues affected this remarkable woman's fiction.
Generously illustrated, this book offers lively new perspectives on the intriguing world of
nineteenth-century Louisiana and especially its famous city, New Orleans.*
—Dr. Barbara Ewell, professor emerita, Loyola University New Orleans;
Kate Chopin scholar

*I have followed Rory and Rosary's New Orleans history books on Degas and Voodoo,
and I am intrigued by how they paint the life of their heroine, Kate Chopin, in all its
shocking and revealing detail. They are writers who don't shy from the real, hard truths
of life in New Orleans at difficult periods of time.*
—Mark Duplass, actor, writer, producer

*There has been much academic research on Kate Chopin, but this book pieces together a
personal portrait of the author and her times—based on scholarly research—that reads
more like compelling popular fiction. This book helps readers to feel that they know Kate
Chopin personally, which is an admirable feat.*
—Dr. C.W. Cannon, professor, Loyola University New Orleans

*Rory O'Neill Schmitt and Rosary O'Neill have given readers a precious gift. We get
to experience Kate Chopin's world through her own eyes—the challenges of being an
independent spirit during Victorian times. Added to that are an abundance of images
that truly set the stage. And a surprise to many will be the connection with family
members of renowned French Impressionist Edgar Degas, who had their own trials and
tribulations in post–Civil War New Orleans.*
—Peggy Scott Laborde, author,
Emmy Award–winning New Orleans public television producer

*Rosary and Rory's writing is remarkably intelligent and intricately lush. With their
opulent and extraordinary verbiage, they manage to judiciously weave beautiful tapestries
of storytelling.*
—Bryan Batt, actor

KATE CHOPIN
in New Orleans

Rory O'Neill Schmitt, PhD, and Rosary O'Neill, PhD

Foreword by Mark Duplass

THE
History
PRESS

Published by The History Press
Charleston, SC
www.historypress.com

First published 2024

Manufactured in the United States

ISBN 9781467157063

Library of Congress Control Number: 2023950466

Notice: The information in this book is true and complete to the best of our knowledge. It is offered without guarantee on the part of the authors or The History Press. The authors and The History Press disclaim all liability in connection with the use of this book.

CONTENTS

Foreword, by Mark Duplass   9
Preface   11

PART I. KATE CHOPIN IN NEW ORLEANS
1. The Fighting Infant, the Troubled Child   15
2. Newlywed to Newly Fled   26
3. Lying In, Dreaming Out   39
4. Degas Is Here!   55
5. Bridge, Battle, Birth   67
6. Cloochy-what? How Do You Even Pronounce It?   82
7. Bayou Secrets, Bayou Pain   96
8. Missouri Shock   111
9. Phoenix Rising   118
10. Strong Wings   128

PART II. MORE SECRETS ABOUT KATE CHOPIN
1. We Just Can't Let You Go, Kate!   137
2. The Soul of an Artist: Poetry by Barret O'Brien   138
3. Experts Reflect on the Chopin Mysteries   141
    Dr. Thomas Bonner, Xavier University   141
    Dr. C.W. Cannon, Loyola University New Orleans   146
    Dr. Barbara Ewell, Loyola University New Orleans   151
    Dr. Bernard Koloski, Mansfield University   158
    Dr. Heidi Podlasli-Labrenz, Independent Chopin Scholar,
        Germany   164

4. Historians Discuss Nineteenth-Century Fashion   160
   Hope Hanafin, Costume Designer for Film   168
   Dr. Linda Welters, Fashion Historian, University
      of Rhode Island   173
5. New Orleanians Converse about Kate Chopin Films   180
   Dr. Barbara Ewell and Rachel Grissom   180
6. Heirs Ponder Legacies   183
   Great-Grandchildren of Kate Chopin   183
   Descendant of Edgar Degas   196
7. More Discoveries about Kate   198
   Margaret Munch, RSCJ, Academy of the Sacred Heart   198
   The Art of the Diary   200
8. Remember Me: A Timeline of Kate Chopin and Louisiana   202
9. Goodbye, Kate. Live On!   210

Acknowledgements   213
Notes   217
About the Authors   223

FOREWORD

by Mark Duplass

New Orleans.

So I'm from New Orleans. And I have a complicated relationship with the place. Because I did all the things. I got drunk way too early and threw up Jell-O shots near the epic mansions on Esplanade. I rode my bike under the weeping oak trees and wrote ridiculously romantic and nostalgic songs and plays that I'll never show anyone. I snuck in to see Jazz at Snug Harbor without paying the cover, and I ate so many beignets as the sun came up over the winding Mississippi River. Yes, that all happened. It's not a fairy tale. That place is real. And I loved it all so much. But then I left.

Like New Orleans mother-daughter authors Rory and Rosary, I too feel a deep connection with the city. But unlike them, I haven't found a way to honor the place in my art. Rory and Rosary are always dipping their toes back into this mysterious place. They understand what it's like to live there, to return there and to celebrate the wonderful and terrible things to be had there.

Louisiana, sometimes forgotten, has seduced artists for centuries. You can see it and feel it in their works. Sometimes it rings true. Sometimes it feels a bit more stock and pandering. Descriptions of the lush foliage of swamps and bayous, French cuisine, jazz music, moonlit balconies, Creole cottages with twenty-foot ceilings and private courtyards, etc. All of these things are true. They exist. But it takes a delicate touch to depict them with authenticity—with the light and the dark.

I went to Jesuit High School. I say this because locals in this small big town are always categorized by where we went to school. Locals like to know everybody, especially everybody they should have come in contact with. Fortunately for me, I went to school with Barret O'Brien, Rosary's son, and so I have had a connection with their family for years. And I have followed Rory and Rosary's New Orleans history books on Degas and Voodoo, and I am intrigued by how they paint the life of their heroine, Kate Chopin, in all its shocking and revealing detail. They are writers who don't shy from the real, hard truths of life in New Orleans at difficult periods of time. They

Courtesy of Duplass Brothers Productions.

are writers who show how grit—well managed—can lead to glory. They are writers who celebrate the victim turned victor, the heroes and heroines of New Orleans' past.

In this intriguing nonfiction book about Kate Chopin's life in Louisiana, Rory and Rosary are remarkable in their ability to capture Kate's story in midair and flesh it out. Kate, a St. Louis debutante turned world-shaker, arrived in New Orleans as a passionate newlywed, adored the city and stayed for over a decade. She fell in love with Louisiana and mesmerized the world with what she knew. Kate would write about New Orleans and Natchitoches in her stories for the rest of her life. She helped push Louisiana into immortality. In a place so quixotic that everyone thinks they can be king or queen of something, there are the exceptional ones, like Kate Chopin, who excel in impossible circumstances—and in doing so, possibly inspire us to do the same.

PREFACE

Who was Kate Chopin—this pioneer, this mother of six, this disciplined wife who wouldn't stop perfecting her intellect and soul, despite the blows of outrageous misfortune?

We, your authors, are cradle New Orleanians, artists, scholars. Growing up, we had no idea that Kate Chopin (1850–1904) also lived in New Orleans. Did you?

New Orleans has its dark underbelly, and the stars were not aligned when Kate moved here. What happened? Every possible shock. How Kate sidestepped and leapfrogged over them is what this book is about. Her fierceness led to her glory as a writer. Trailblazers do just that—prepare the way.

We have lived as insiders and outsiders (New York/California/Arizona). We have been admired and shamed for our New Orleans accents. Discounted as too smart or too stupid. Included and excluded.

We have loved and left the city and been haunted to return. It is hard to escape the intoxicating Big Easy, where family woos, warms and welcomes. How could anyone leave Louisiana? Gumbo, crawfish bisque, crabmeat au gratin. Jazz parades, dancing in the streets, lavender nights. Creole cottages in popsicle colors, streets lined with mama oak trees, steamboats on the huge wild Mississippi River. A place where people still sit on their porches and talk into the night. A town where anything difficult should be postponed for family or fun. "Don't study too hard; it could mess up your brain."

Daughters of New Orleans, we've authored books on our beloved city (*Edgar Degas in New Orleans, New Orleans Voodoo: A Cultural History* and *New Orleans Carnival Krewes: The History, Spirit and Secrets of Mardi Gras*). Louisiana, the land of blooming festivities, also exists as the cove of decaying dreams.

Like Kate, we have been bewitched and endangered both by charmers and predators. We've dodged hairy caterpillars dangling from oak trees, swatted vampiric mosquitos, watched hurricanes puncture roofs and flatten palm trees. New Orleanians have survived the bitter for the beautiful.

When we show you the homes in Kate's neighborhoods, we've seen them, stood wide-eyed at their failed grandeur, their twenty-five-foot ceilings, their balconies of wrought iron, their wraparound porches—all the voluptuous details that cry out for maintenance.

Kate landed with a passionate curiosity for all she could see and feel in this land of fibrous bayous and violent sun where God cries through the never-ending rain.

Something in the grit of Louisiana pushed Kate to make her own rules here, steel past mediocrity and develop defiant independence. Few know what propels a wife to defy custom, peek outside the cage, resist the leash. At first, many locals sneeringly accepted her. Kate was wealthy, eccentric, on fire—something that the rich in New Orleans secretly admired. Though many locals didn't quite "get" Kate, they stomached her idiosyncrasies. She was a "good wife" and soon-to-be mother. If her Creole husband put up with her, so could they.

Kate was protected, or so she thought.

Kate's story is worth telling because of the magnitude of her victory over shame and silencing. This book studies the genius behind her seeming "madness" and defiant writing, the betrayals that drove her to flee Louisiana yet write about it all her life as if she was writing it out of herself.

Louisiana wrenched Kate's heart and sent her to her writing desk, a sanctuary for her deep private joy and agony. She spoke her truth, and in so doing, she spoke ours and became one of the first great American authors.

Let us lure you, dear reader, to Louisiana, with its lush foliage, barbaric heat, suicide oaks and furious hurricanes. The guts and grandeur of the times will haunt you, and you'll start to feel the joy, the grief, the everything in between that Kate did, as her experiences here, we believe, launched her writing career.

We, your New Orleans authors, humbly salute you. "Hear, hear, Kate Chopin!"

PART I

◇ ◇ ◇

KATE CHOPIN
IN NEW ORLEANS

Chapter 1

THE FIGHTING INFANT, THE TROUBLED CHILD

I am diametrically opposed to parties and balls and yet when I broach the subject—they either laugh at me—imagining that I wish to perpetrate a joke; or look very serious, shake their heads and tell me not to encourage such silly notions.[1]
—Kate Chopin

Katherine O'Flaherty[2] arrived in this world defiant. What made her so determined to survive while so many wee ones in 1850 died before the age of five? Did Kate not feel her mother tremble as she tiptoed around the house at the end of her confinement? Oh, if only Kate could be the healthy baby her mother yearned for.

Kate's mother likely cried out for joy, longing for a link to femininity. Eliza had been married for six years to a rich Irish immigrant widower—who came with a four-year-old son—and she had given birth to another son. But Kate was her first daughter.

Eliza came from a line of strong French women, aristocrats, now impoverished. Her Thomas O'Flaherty (thirty-nine) had pushed his way to wealth by starting a boat store, a wholesale grocery and a commission house in St. Louis. He'd buried one wife (age twenty-four) and their newborn. And he'd remarried six months later, to Kate's mother (age sixteen).

Kate likely hooked antlers with her Papa from Galway. Some say Kate, irascible, got on his nerves, and so he locked her away in boarding school. Catholic nuns at the Academy of the Sacred Heart would tame her. Being wrenched from her mother (and siblings—fifteen, seven and two) must have

Left: Eliza O'Flaherty with her stepson, George (1840–1859). George's mother, Catherine de Reilhe, and brother died in childbirth in 1844, and his father remarried Eliza six months later. *Missouri Historical Society.*

Right: Eliza Faris O'Flaherty, Kate Chopin's mother. *Missouri Historical Society.*

Thomas O'Flaherty and Eliza Faris O'Flaherty, Kate Chopin's parents. *Missouri Historical Society.*

Left: Portrait of Kate O'Flaherty as a child. *Missouri Historical Society.*

Right: Victoire Verdon, wife of Joseph C. Charleville, great-grandmother of Kate Chopin (and her first teacher). *Missouri Historical Society.*

felt more like an execution to a five-year-old, even if boarding school was customary for the elite.

Did Kate cry under the sheets at night, tormented she'd be forgotten like so many orphans shunted by cholera or a fire? As nuns closed a sheet around her bed at night, did Kate breathe a quick prayer that her life might go out? No mother to confide in, no brothers to look up to, no relative to amuse. Was little Kate dreaming of how she could escape? In convents like that, German shepherds were released at night to run the grounds, scaring off intruders. Whenever little Kate went home for a visit, we imagine, her father sent her promptly back. A busy, important founder of the Missouri Pacific Railroad, he had to plan for his inaugural train ride to open the St. Louis route.

In November 1855, everyone thought train travel was safe. But a freak accident on the train killed thirty passengers, one of them Kate's dad.

Tragedy brought sorrow and freedom. Twenty-seven-year-old Eliza scooped up her daughter (five and a half). Now Eliza stood at the helm of her rich household, beholden to no man. A widow could control the family money till she remarried (but Eliza never would).

Ladies' and children's clothing (late 1850s). *Illustration from the University of Rhode Island's Historic Textile and Costume Collection.*

Believing education could heal, Eliza aimed to fill the family's anguish of death with knowledge. She brought her mother and grandmother, strong and independent widows, on board to give Kate individual instruction. Like the nuns of the day school at Sacred Heart, family mentors taught Kate to live a life of the mind, as well as a life of the home. They tutored Kate, as only the disciplined French can, coaching her with daily piano and French lessons and quenching her sorrow in the deep emotional expressiveness of language in books.

Cocooned in her family, did Kate miss her father? Do girls ever forget their fathers, especially ones who die overnight? Do cruelty and indifference vanish when a face is frozen in memory? She never really got to tell her father goodbye.

Kate lived in a time of broken hearts and crushed dreams. Many girls lived in dread of pregnancy. So many mothers died in childbirth and so many daughters and sons through disease. In the 1850s, one in four children didn't even make it to their tenth birthday.[3]

Sudden deaths had robbed Kate of her younger sisters, Marie Thérèse and Jennie, who died at infancy and age three. Did Kate worry how many Christmases she had left?

GIRL WRITER

Writing became Kate's healing elixir. Even at ten, she kept a diary, a Christmas gift from her aunt, who keenly perceived Kate's interest in writing and drawing. Journaling strengthened Kate's perception and ignited her imagination. Diaries and letters were the only outlets for girls to document,

Left: Kate Chopin's copybook, titled "Leaves of Affection" (1860–69). This bird drawing recalls a future line she'd write, "The bird that would soar above the level plane of tradition and prejudice must have strong wings." *Missouri Historical Society.*

Right: Kitty Garesché, Kate Chopin's best friend (1870). *Missouri History Museum.*

Kate O'Flaherty, Kitty Garesché and Lily Garesché (1866), Academy of Sacred Heart, City House, St. Louis, Missouri. *Image courtesy of the Academy of Sacred Heart Archives, Missouri.*

reflect, think freely, fantasize. A home for her intense feelings, the diary protected Kate's surging creativity.

Young Kate wrote in her journal:

Oh! It is such a joy in youth to be alone with one's daydreams.

She even invited her close friend, Kitty Gareshé (who would later become a nun), to inscribe in her book.

In 1860, Kate wrote:

Let this album be dedicated to friendship. Make it an altar where every pure offering of affection be laid. Let the thought herein inscribed be as untainted as the snowflake; each wish so pure and bright as the sun beams of Heaven.

Writing inside the academy was a haven for Kate, though she did not know of worse horrors approaching. Outside of St. Louis, the country was unravelling, festering into war.

WAR IN HER FRONT YARD

Did Kate know what a civil war was when it hit her world when she was eleven? Would you have?

How could Kate have guessed that amid all the chaos, half of St. Louis was defending the North and half the South?

When Kate waved off her soldier half brother, did she fear he wouldn't return?

George's death was Kate's first bite into the poisoned apple of war. The year 1863 also saw the death of her great-grandmother and the banishment of her best friend.

Did young Kate scream herself to sleep at the impermanence of life? Still, she had to be sewn into mourning clothes, wear them for six months and watch her mother, in crepe mourning attire, retreat from social contact.

Grieving for her brother, did Kate enjoy ripping down a Union flag that soldiers had hung on her porch? She couldn't fling her despondent self at her mother or her older brother, Tom Jr., the only sibling she had left. True, her wee sisters had died, but girls weren't supposed to bury their brothers on Mardi Gras Day in some far-off place like Arkansas.

HEALING KATE'S HEART, GROWING KATE'S MIND

Kate returned to the solace of nuns at Sacred Heart day school (when it was safe enough to reopen). She may not have realized that she was being educated by some of the greatest minds in St. Louis. They soothed her by focusing on her intellectual development through literature, German and French languages, music.

Honing her compositions, young Kate found healing. She wrote,

> *How then express the grief with which we follow the young, the gifted, the beautiful to the silent tomb?*

Kate would bring all that breathtaking knowledge with her to troubled New Orleans when she moved there just a few years later. Covering her sorrows with gold medals for art, music, history, English, French—for everything—she would graduate with honors. And she was, thank God, pretty: a necessary blessing in a time when many placed a woman's value on her looks.

DEFIANT DEBUTANTE

As Kate bloomed, her family worried. At nineteen, her beauty years were slipping behind her. She would be an "old maid" after twenty-two. The ripe time for marriage started at sixteen (her mother's age when she wed her much older father.)

Nuns had trained Kate and her debutante classmates in the fine art of conversation. Now it was time to put that into practice.

Eliza insisted Kate display herself in a debut in St. Louis.[4] Kate learned how to waltz, how to dine with grace, how to wear long gloves and remove them with one hand, how to walk with a swan neck and step with light feet, how to lift a voluminous skirt and dance as if spinning on a cloud. Unknowingly, Kate had been trained to be the jewel on the arm of a powerful man.

But Kate hated the artificial rituals, which stole her from reading and writing. How could she stomach constricting herself in a ballgown, wining and dining with "debutante delights" (the tongue-in-cheek name for hand-picked males looking for wives)? Yes, there was a list made by the debutante committee.

But questioning social customs, even playfully, was completely unacceptable. Kate begrudgingly participated:

> *I am a creature who loves amusements; I love brightness and gaiety and life and sunshine. But is it a rational amusement, I ask myself, to destroy one's health, and turn night into day? I look about me, though, and see persons so much better than myself, and so much more pious engaging in the self-same pleasures—however, I fancy it cannot have the same effect upon them as it does upon me.—Heigh ho!*
>
> *I wish this were the only subject I have doubts upon. One does become so tired—reasoning, reasoning, reasoning from morning till night and coming to no conclusions—it is to say the least, slightly unsatisfactory.*

Disgruntled, Kate twirled and curtsied in the ballroom. The music lover, Francophile, intellectual complained in her diary:

> *What a nuisance all this is—I wish it were over. I write in my book today the first time for months; parties, operas, concerts, skating and amusements ad infinitum have so taken up all my time that my dear reading and writing that I love so well have suffered much neglect.*

We wonder if Kate even wanted to become a wife and a mother. Maybe not, but what were her options? A cloistered nun or a mother-woman? Kate pressed on a smile and shielded herself:

> *A friend who knows me as well as anyone is capable of knowing me—a gentleman of course—told me that I had a way in conversation of discovering a person's characteristics—opinions and private feelings—while they knew no more about me at the end than they knew at the beginning of the conversation....*
>
> *I feel as though I should like to run away and hide myself; but there is no escaping....*
>
> *All required of you is to have control over the muscles of your face—to look pleased and chagrined, surprised indignant and under every circumstance—interested and entertained. Lead your antagonist to talk about himself—he will not enter reluctantly upon the subject I assure you—and 20 to one—he will report to you as one of the most entertaining and intelligent persons,—although the whole extent of your conversation was but an occasional "What did you say?" "What did you do?"—"What do you think?"...*

I'm invited to a ball and I go. I dance with people I despise; amuse myself with men whose only talent lies in their feet; gain the disapprobation of people I honor and respect; return home at daybreak with my brain in the state which was never intended for it; and arise in the middle of the next day feeling infinitely more, in spirit and flesh like a Liliputian, than a woman with a body and soul.

Kate likely found most of the suitors to be boors, poorly intentioned, blind to her intelligence with little interest in her inner soul. Oh, how she would have loved to have dismissed them all!

SPELLBOUND

But one suitor spied her when she gracefully came out in high society. Equally refined, he enjoyed seeing her at his Uncle Louis Benoist's Oakland house, a 476-acre Italian estate. Maybe he watched her move gracefully on the dance floor, corseted, petticoated in rich silks, an abundance of bows and ribbons, a voluminous skirt.

He was a wealthy Creole businessman, a virile twenty-six. Polished, well-read, discriminatingly schooled in the ways of love. And did we mention he was French? It was rumored that soon, he would be inheriting a massive family estate in Louisiana.

To top it off, he was from New Orleans, a city of dreams, which Kate "liked immensely" (according to her journal). The city had bewitched Kate in 1869 when she visited with her mother. How she had loved the evening she spent at that home near Esplanade Strect:

I quaffed all sorts of ale and ices—talked French and German—listened enchanted to Mrs. Bader's exquisite singing and for two or three hours was as gay and happy as I ever have been in my life.

Kate likely fantasized about living in New Orleans, a metropolis filled with starlit boat cruises and a poetic Garden District shaded by drooping oak trees. Did she daydream of one day living in a mansion decorated with canopied bedrooms?

Kate kept her electric connection with her New Orleans suitor a secret. We imagine that he gave her space to breathe and set ablaze her soul's freedom. Their engagement was only whispered between the pages of her journal.

New Orleans historic home, interior. *Photograph by Cheryl Gerber.*

Pitot House, interior bedroom. *Photograph by Rachelle O'Brien.*

Exactly one year has elapsed since my book and I held intercourse, and what changes have occurred! Not so much outwardly as within. My book has been shut up in a great immense chest buried under huge folios through which I could never penetrate, and I—have not missed it. Pardon me, my friend, but I never flatter you.

All that has transpired between then and now vanishes before this one consideration—in two weeks I am going to be married; married to the right man. It does not seem strange as I thought it would—I feel perfectly calm, perfectly collected. And how surprised everyone was, for I had kept it so secret!

And who was this New Orleanian who swept Kate off her feet? Aurelian Roselius Oscar Chopin.

Chapter 2

NEWLYWED TO NEWLY FLED

Oscar riveted Kate with his intense gaze, full lips, thick hair swept to the side. Oscar could drive a horse or steer a bank, speak perfect French. A whole town in northern Louisiana, Chopinville, was named after his family. He applauded Kate's bold stance. She tickled his sense of the outrageous, with her cigar in hand (unthinkable for a woman).

I Do

On her wedding day, June 9, 1870, did Kate, twenty, awake breathlessly, questions bubbling up about the thrilling intimacies ahead on their European honeymoon? She journaled:

> *My wedding day! How simple it is to say and how hard to realize that I am married, no longer a young lady with nothing to think of but myself and nothing to do.*
>
> *We went to holy Communion this morning, my mother with us, and it gave me a double happiness to see so many of my friends at mass for I knew they prayed for me on this happiest day of my life.*
>
> *The whole day seems like a dream to me; how I awoke early in the morning before the household was stirring and looked out of the window to see whether the sun would shine or not; how I went to mass and could not read the prayers in my book; afterwards, how I dressed for my*

Oscar Chopin and Kate O'Flaherty at the time of their marriage (1870). *Missouri Historical Society.*

marriage—went to church and found myself married before I could think what I was doing.

St. Louis celebrated Kate and Oscar in the newspaper: "Still Another Marriage in Fashionable Society."

WILD WEDDING TRIP

The world was a luscious apple, and Kate was taking her first bite—not knowing how venomous it might be. Did excitement, distance or youth blind Kate and Oscar to the nightmares lying ahead?

Oh, how quickly Kate was pulled onto the ship that summer. Didn't she sense any tension when she boarded the German vessel, the *Rhein*, headed for Germany? No, she was giggling inside feeling herself birthed a new woman, a wife, when people called her "Mrs. Chopin" and not "Miss Katy." The Franco-Prussian War was brewing, but Kate was starry-

A bakery in Germany sells *Käsekuchen* (cheesecakes), tarts, carrot cake and *Schwarzwälder Kirschtorte* (black forest cake). *Photograph by Insiah Zaidi.*

eyed arriving in Germany, noting in her honeymoon journal, "The private residences are the most exquisite little gems, and the people all look so amiable and happy."

Soon they were having tea with Oscar's business associate, Mr. Knoop, the tycoon of Bremen, in the princeliest private residence that the couple had ever seen, "a miracle of costliness and exquisite taste." They relished delicious cakes, like *Käsekuchen*, *Schwarzwälder Kirschtorte* and *Apfelkuchen*.

Was Oscar securing contacts for his father's cotton empire? Or was he postwar naïve? He'd been succeeding in St. Louis in his uncle's bank. Did he believe New Orleans cotton was booming in Europe? Was that why the Germans were so friendly?

Kate shrugged off any misgivings, dazzle-eyed, sipping Rhine wine and nibbling strawberries, visiting gardens, horseback riding, sailing boats, smoking cigars and taking long walks. She began shopping, purchasing Brussels and Valenciennes linens in anticipation of New Orleans housekeeping, "which awaits me on the 'other side.'"

But Kate's first wake-up slap came in Bonn, where Germans banned her from seeing the student halls at the university because she was female. When

The University of Bonn is formally known as Rheinische-Friedrich-Wilhelms Universität Bonn. *Photograph by Insiah Zaidi.*

The Pantheon, Paris. *Photograph by Rachelle O'Brien.*

Kate protested that she was an uninterested, married woman, her argument didn't land. Even in Germany, women faced physical and metaphorical closed doors.

Whispers of the Franco-Prussian War rocketed to screams. Residents and tourists scattered like rodents scurrying underground. War threatened where Kate and Oscar could go and when. Baden was off the table; Paris was a maybe. If only they had traveled directly to New Orleans and not gone to Europe!

Opposite: Hofgarten is a popular place for student hangouts at the University of Bonn. *Photograph by Insiah Zaidi.*

Left: A Parisian park. *Photograph by Rachelle O'Brien.*

Below: Tuileries Garden, Paris. *Photograph by Rachelle O'Brien.*

Opposite, top: An alley in Paris. *Photograph by Rory O'Neill Schmitt, PhD.*

Opposite, bottom: La Madeleine Church, exterior, Paris. *Photograph by Rachelle O'Brien.*

Above: La Madeleine Church, interior, Paris. *Photograph by Rachelle O'Brien.*

Weeks after their wedding, Kate and Oscar were confined in an empty hotel. Kate literally bumped into the commander in chief of the Prussian army, Von Moltke, in a stairwell. Nothing seized their attention but war news. How to get out and get to New Orleans?

In Paris, Kate learned that the French were being defeated on every side. An appeal from headquarters begged all men capable of bearing arms to try to save France.

Kate and Oscar found solace at Mass in La Madeleine Church. When they exited the church steps, Kate witnessed thousands crying, "Vive la République!" Kate wrote:

> *I have seen a French Revolution! We have seen the rude populace running and strutting through the private grounds of the Tuileries: places that 24 hours ago were looked upon as almost sacred ground.*

In September 1870, while Parisians were burning down trees, Kate and Oscar made it onto one of the last trains that left Paris for Brest; then the terrified couple boarded a steamer to New York. Oscar probably comforted Kate on the perilous passage. He knew how to please women, and please Kate he did, and pregnant she became.

New Home: New Orleans

But anxieties didn't end when landing in New Orleans. As soon as Kate set up housekeeping in their new double on Magazine Street, she had to appease her troubled French father-in-law. An irascible fifty-seven-year-old, Jean Baptiste hadn't been feeling well and had written a will, but he may have been disposed to think the malady was less serious as a few weeks passed. Kate distracted him from his reclusive abode on Royal Street, appeased him in their new home by singing and playing French songs on the piano (not knowing he was actually dying).

Kate probably feared to tell Jean Baptiste that she was expecting. A doctor, he knew the dangers of infection for her and the unborn child. He was grieving his wife, who had died of typhoid weeks before Oscar's wedding.

Jean Baptiste fueled anxiety in his son, had pressured him to learn the international cotton business. The two had a stormy relationship, and as the old man weakened, tension ignited. Some said the ruthless doctor was an inspiration for Harriet Beecher Stowe's book *Uncle Tom's Cabin*. He'd tortured enslaved laborers and exploited colleagues before the Civil War, dominating his business like a monster. Would Oscar follow suit?

Oh, it was all too awful. Had the nuns taught Kate tactics for managing tyranny?

In October, typhoid struck Jean Baptiste with violence. The worst manifestations occurred: persistently high fever, rash, severe abdominal discomfort, intestinal bleeding. Jean Baptiste, the French-trained physician, impermeable to pain, was weakening day by day. Then, one day in November, his soul sailed to God.

Did Kate witness Jean Baptiste's shocking death, perhaps terrified she would succumb to typhoid, too? Some said typhoid was contagious and the stricken carried the bacteria in their bloodstream and intestinal tract. Others explained unsanitary conditions in New Orleans hastened typhoid's spread.

The Catholic funeral procession marched forward with a lavish Mass at St. Louis Cathedral, and Jean Baptiste was buried next to his wife (whom he was known to have battered ruthlessly), in St. Louis Cemetery No. 3. Kate, in shock, was sewn into black crepe almost overnight.

THE ELDEST SON

A viciously run cotton empire was thrust into the arms of gentle Oscar, the eldest son, twenty-seven. Would he know how to lead it?

Oscar began negotiating steamer tickets to sail back to war-torn Paris, a place he had barely left. Ships sank mid-ocean, especially when high winds and tidal waves prevailed. And they did in hurricane season, which it was. What else was Oscar to do? He couldn't settle his father's accounts by long-to-arrive letters. No time for explanation. Kate would have to get used to this new life, where wives took the blows of outrageous fortune and sudden absence.

If Kate wasn't pregnant, she might have accompanied him, soothing herself with chocolates, oranges and forbidden cigars in the Hotel Bergère.

Maybe Oscar promised Kate that he'd be back soon with golden pockets. Oscar was charming French, and Kate had lived in a rather insular world in Missouri. Now the man whom wide-eyed Kate had moved to Louisiana for was gone. Gone to handle his dead father's affairs in Paris. Gone.

Kate lived alone craving a letter, fearing a telegram. She became a journal wife, whispering her fears into the little lock-and-key diary hidden under a pillow or in a pocket.

AN ORPHAN'S GUARDIAN

And then another shocker in the form of an unwanted child was dropped at her door. Kate was selected to care for Oscar's orphaned nine-year-old sister. His siblings, miles away, refused to do it. Oscar's sister Eugenie, twenty-three, was already burdened with four children from her husband's first marriage. Oscar's kid brother, Lamy, twenty-one, was a happy self-absorbed bachelor, building his fortune.

No matter that the little girl had been raised on her parents' 4,367-acre estate upriver near the siblings. No matter that within eighteen months, the child had buried both parents.

Did Kate hear the child cry herself to sleep, fight off demons in nightmarish dreams, wail and pound the pillow with fistfuls of sorrow? How did Kate console this girl, who could have stood ghostlike at the foot of Kate's bed, desolate in black mourning attire? Kate probably realized that if she didn't nurture her, the girl might lie down and die.

The abandoned Kate reached out to the abandoned Marie. They endured together, folding inside each other's sorrow. Marie felt Kate's loneliness. Kate felt Marie's shocked grief.

Mule wagon stuck in street, New Orleans (1884–85).
Photograph by Edward Wilson. The Historic New Orleans Collection.

Left: Fashion plate depicting crinolines (1860). *Illustration from the University of Rhode Island's Historic Textile and Costume Collection.*

Below: Esplanade Avenue homes, New Orleans. *Photograph by Rachelle O'Brien.*

Childhood deaths had stricken Kate at five (her father) and thirteen (her brother). Death lingered as an ever-present and unmentionable threat. Both Kate and Marie probably worried they'd get typhoid through infected water, food or God knows what. Even Queen Victoria's husband had been flattened by typhoid, despite a galaxy of doctors.

Girl-mothers, like Kate, isolated themselves in mansions, surrounded by shivering palms and drooping banana trees in New Orleans, confined to loneliness in the bedroom, on the porch, on the front balcony. Pregnant Creole women were often kept apart and lived terrified. They couldn't reach for an alarm or the reins of a carriage to drive. They weren't even supposed to run or shout.

Perhaps Kate and Marie, confined mostly to the house and shrouded in black, distracted each other.

Maybe Kate, a debutante just the year prior, taught the child the art of twisting, pearl inlaying or ribbon braiding the hair. Perhaps she showed her how to cinch a shoulder-to-hip corset and strap on horsehair crinolines with metal bands.

Kate likely drew back the lace curtains, looked out the window, ogled the world on Magazine Street peacocking by. Long walks would have been impossible for many months, unless Kate violated decorum rules. A grieving orphan and a wife who'd lost both her mother-in-law and father-in-law and was obviously pregnant had better not be seen in public.

Desperate spectators, Kate and Marie probably critiqued the women who passed. Ladies in pale white, blue, gray, lilac and pink tottered forward under hats and veils, which both protected them from the sun and impaired their vision. No doubt the ladies giggled at the hats trimmed with ribbons, flowers or feathers that tilted ladies forward, colluding with the sweaty cobblestones to fell them. Maybe Kate played with Marie's hair, coiling it around her finger under a tilting hat with a veil, like the imperiled walkers. But for male escorts, the women would be blind ducks walking toward a cliff.

Kate likely wondered how would she befriend New Orleans, exist as a free, independent thinker-doer, if she was escort-dependent or always cloistered with a child. Did she dare go out?

Chapter 3

LYING IN, DREAMING OUT

We suspect Kate thought a lot about being trapped as a woman, alone as she was with that nine-year-old girl. She hardly knew Oscar's country relatives and wasn't sure she wanted to. Would they visit after the cotton season ended in November 1870? Didn't they know she was young, pregnant, alone? Were they still annoyed Oscar married someone from a state that had not seceded from the Union?

As Kate's belly expanded, did she dream of going back to St. Louis to give birth in a town she knew? Trains were slow and bumpy (twenty-two miles an hour); the river was full of desperadoes and scavengers. Yellow fever, scarlet fever and typhoid abounded in port cities, like New Orleans. Who knew what made diseases fester, travel through the air? Was it even safe to go outside? Travel was dangerous with infections multiplying in crowds.

Could Kate's mother drop her St. Louis responsibilities and trek to New Orleans? Eliza had so many people depending on her in St. Louis: Kate's brother, grandmother, aunts and uncles. Kate had to accept becoming a mother, apart from all her family and friends. She had to brace herself for the possible nightmare of a sick child: riding in a buggy with a feverish infant or sending notes to the few remaining medical professionals in town. Many of them had died in the war or fled.

Kate probably hadn't thought through the disaster of being seven hundred miles away from everyone she loved. Probably a consoling letter from her brother, Tom, would take weeks to arrive.

Left: Kate O'Flaherty before her marriage to Oscar Chopin (1860–69). *Missouri Historical Society.*

Below: Charity Hospital. *Photograph by George Mugnier. Louisiana State Museum.*

Crisis in Confinement

Back then, women gave birth screaming, without drugs or knowledge of what was to come. Cautionary mothers, sisters, midwives surrounded the lucky. Would Kate find a doctor and get chloroform? Queen Victoria (mother of nine) had used the new drug for her childbirths.

Kate probably tried to read about childbirth, but it wasn't spoken about in most novels, stories or poems. Kate, just twenty, would ride out her pregnancy soon enough, and she hoped childbirth wouldn't compromise or kill her as it had so many.

Mothers and children died every day, and no one knew what caused it. An infant casket in a Garden District home would be loaded and slipped through a side door, newly installed to protect family members from public sorrow.

With no guide, how did Kate deal with fear? Certainly not by unloading on the already traumatized Marie. Did Kate hold her tongue, puff a cigar, sneak out for a walk around the block?

The Baby Comes

1871

Endless days of hoping and despairing passed—and then somehow, that spring, double blessings. Twenty-seven-year-old Oscar made it back to New Orleans after months in Paris. And Kate's mother was beside her. (Oscar wasn't allowed in the birthing room.)

The rage of labor was ripping through Kate, but finally, the newborn came hurtling out, screaming strong. All the terrors associated with childbirth soared, then vanished. Kate wrote:

> *I can remember yet that hot southern day on Magazine St. in New Orleans. The noises of the street coming through the open windows; that heaviness with which I dragged myself about; my husband's and mother's solicitude; old Alexandrine, the quadroon nurse, with her high bandana tignon, her hoop-earrings and placid smile; old Dr. Faget; the smell of chloroform....*
>
> *Waking at 6 in the evening, from out of a stupor, to see in my mother's arms a little piece of humanity all dressed in white, which they told me*

was my little son! The sensation with which I touched my lips and my fingertips to his soft flesh only comes once to a mother, it must be the pure animal sensation: nothing spiritual could be so real—so poignant.

Born on May 22, 1871, Jean-Baptiste was named after his French grandfather (perhaps to reverse the curse). Everyone was jubilant. What could possibly go wrong? But this was New Orleans, and of course, something did.

LOUISIANA MAMA

Things were happy with Kate's mother, Eliza, forty-three, spinning about, showing Kate how to care for, soothe and feed a newborn. But then she departed. Like an angel, she floated away.

Oscar had been Kate's exceptional man-guide—brilliant, sensitive, strong—but he was gone a lot, securing the cotton office, his inheritance, his rural properties, his whatever. He was desperately sorting out his father's cotton business, which he hadn't planned to steer. With no one to lead him, Oscar was in a rudderless situation, and so was Kate. He likely returned home a husk with whom she ate and slept.

Who would Kate confide in? Women usually whispered their secrets to their mothers, sisters, their compatriots in woe. What could Kate do but become an old, wise woman at twenty-one, propping herself and her newborn up in bed? Semi-clothed, facing a blistering summer confinement alone? She couldn't surrender, die, whine herself to sleep; telegraph her mother a ten-word emergency; count on the nine-year-old orphan lolling nearby to help her.

June 1871 was hot, hot in Louisiana. Kate was sweating all over with so few baths—one per week at best. All she could do was sigh, groan or scream within herself. She pulled out one breast, then another, to feed the teeny, squirming baby. A first-time mom, she was trying to get by like so many, grateful for three hours of sleep.

Carte de visite of a young woman (1860s). Louisiana ladies often shared calling cards on visiting days, like this example from Massachusetts. *From the University of Rhode Island's Historic Textile and Costume Collection. Photography by J.S. Howard.*

Avoiding depression and pressing on was a challenge. Maybe Kate skimmed a serial novel while breastfeeding, devoured the newspaper for poetry, while patting a baby's back. If only she could soon join a New Orleans literary group or pass around a scandalous Goncourt novel? But she would have to postpone her passions to amuse this orphaned child and keep her infant alive.

Months passed, and local busybodies eventually encouraged Kate to have a weekly reception day. But did Kate enjoy chatting about the latest eye, ear or stomach infection? No, she didn't want to waste her time with vacuous women. Kate likely slipped out before inspecting any calling card on a silver tray. Solitude was better than mindless social calls. But did Oscar mind that Kate wasn't involving herself in the Creole community and strengthening his business possibilities?

No matter that Kate was an intellectual, a skilled musician, a scholar. Inside, didn't she feel she should have some deeper purpose?

CAPTURING KATE

Something Kate had lost reemerged with that strange little girl idling underfoot and with the defenseless infant at her breast. Bravery took hold. She hadn't come this far to be trapped in her bedroom, taking three-hour naps, laying wet cloths over her skin, flinging the window open to let in torrential Louisiana rain.

So what if infections mounted with the Louisiana weather and the weak dropped dead? Who knew how long Kate would be in New Orleans—or even alive? So what if ladies didn't take a train without their husband's written permission, hail a buggy, mount a horse and ride? She was Kate Chopin and would for herself decide.

Once Kate made up her mind to go out, no devil could hold her back.

Kate wanted to walk. Alone. This was something that ladies of her class did not do. Unescorted ladies were punished. They wouldn't be admitted to cafés or hotels. Restaurants were for men who couldn't make it home to eat or wanted to meet colleagues. Unaccompanied women might be rejected, harassed or accosted.

No matter. Something inside Kate might have said: *Go forward*.

Too many thought female independence was a madness. Too few believed assertive women weren't sick. Too easily were eccentric women straitjacketed as lunatics and incompetents. Committal might simply be "by the request of the husband," with no evidence of insanity required.

French Quarter building with a double balcony, New Orleans. *Photograph by Rachelle O'Brien.*

STEPPIN' OUT

Kate started learning New Orleans by seeing it—sneaking out for long solitary walks. She dressed in fashionable walking clothes; she wasn't completely defiant of societal expectations. She was part French, after all.

Oh, what she endured for those walks. A carapace of clothes despite the heat and humidity of the deep South: gartered stockings, pantaloons, hip-length bodices, whalebone corsets, horsehair crinolines, heavy black dresses, stiff bustles and trains and high-buttoned walking shoes. She could barely move her fingers in the too-tight gloves, much less unbutton them to light up a Cuban cigarette. Who made up this rule that no lady went out without gloves? But alas, gloves weren't just for elegance; they also protected against disease.

We imagine Kate stuck a pin through her narrow diadem of a crepe hat, pulled netting over her face. Appearing hatless was like appearing naked. She didn't want rumors to start buzzing about her.

Kate grabbed her small leather purse, hooked her umbrella on her wrist and marched out. If her throat got parched, she'd have to bear it. Drinking water came from contaminated cisterns. One sip could lead to dysentery, cholera, typhoid. On her solitary walks, Kate would have seen grief rituals

Map of New Orleans (1873). *From* Appletons' Hand Book of American Travel, *edited by Charles H. Jones.*

multiplying. Black wreaths were hung, black curtains drawn; women veiled in black answered doors. Bodies piled three high in death carts.

Kate fueled her own creativity and walked the city. There was no father, husband or brother-in-law escorting her. Her brother, Tom, was hundreds of miles away. She would hold herself up, with her strong will, moving forward unescorted, skirt tucked up, umbrella and a little reticule with her cigarettes on her wrist.

Pulling down her glove, she'd light up a smoke. People on the street stared at her. Women didn't smoke in public—much less a beautiful woman at twenty-one—and ladies didn't smoke at all. Kate wouldn't shrink into a shell of who she was supposed to be. Walking was how she found herself in New Orleans in the 1870s. An eager explorer, she gave herself permission to cover as much of the town as she could, later remarking:

> I always feel so sorry for women who don't like to walk; they miss so much—so many rare little glimpses of life; and we women learn so little of life as a whole.

How dare she have fun, amuse herself alone, not spend every waking minute with her family? Kate banked up impressions for future Louisiana stories she would write.

Creole women gazed down from their balconies, those public-private spheres, where the isolated watched: women, confined but complacent, in their garish prisons. The suspicious tagged Kate as peculiar. And some of Oscar's acquaintances made shaming comments about Kate.

The Chopins' address on Magazine Street, between Terpsichore and Robin Streets, was not prestigious, but it was in a neighborhood close to everything, including St. Charles Avenue. Kate took a green car out to City Park and Metairie Cemetery; she'd stop for refreshment in a private garden at the Half-Way House on the Shell Road, where a bustling Creole woman was generous and unconventional with refreshments, midway between the city and Lake Pontchartrain. Kate would smoke whenever the opportunity arose.

She might steer clear of the parish church: St. Patrick's on Camp Street and Girod Street in the Irish Channel area, and head for Canal Street, which divided the American section from the French Quarter.

A long few blocks to the left was where cotton brokers (like Oscar) worked on Union Street and Carondelet, and big blocks to the right had Tchoupitoulas, the levee and the Mississippi River.

Pitot House, balcony. This Louisiana-style bayou house was owned from 1805 to 1810 by Marie Rillieux, the great-grandmother of Edgar Degas. She sold the home to John Pitot, the first elected mayor of New Orleans. *Photograph by Rachelle O'Brien.*

Lower Garden District, New Orleans. *Pen drawing by Billy Harris.*

47

Left: New Orleans. *Photograph by Rachelle O'Brien.*

Below: City Park. *Photograph by Rachelle O'Brien.*

Opposite: St. Patrick's Church, altar. *Photograph by Rachelle O'Brien.*

Kate inhaled the steamships and barges working the riverside and dashed amid the hustle and bustle of the business district. Her travels may appear ordinary to today's reader, unless we keep remembering that many postpartum mothers were imprisoned in their houses.

More and more walks introduced Kate to the blood of the Crescent City. She'd note descriptions of what she saw, especially the colorfully painted

Boats on the Mississippi River, New Orleans. *Photograph by Cheryl Gerber.*

Oscar Chopin, cotton factor and commission merchant, 26 Union Street. A receipt dated April 26, 1873. *Missouri Historical Society.*

Streetcar on St. Charles Avenue. *Photograph by Cheryl Gerber.*

A mule and carriage, New Orleans. *Photograph by Rachelle O'Brien.*

mule cars on Canal Street. She quelled her outsider's anxiety through delightful streetcar rides, car bells jingling and mules' hoofs beating the cobblestones. Kate was getting the hang of the city so that she could write about it with the intimacy of a male local. She described her challenges navigating all seventeen confusing routes in her New Orleans journal: "Was it the green, yellow, or blue car?"

A striking pair of metallic women's boots (c. 1900), made in Lynn, Massachusetts. These boots were exhibited in *Fashioning America: Grit to Glamour* at the New Orleans Museum of Art, 2023. *Photograph by Rachelle O'Brien.*

Kate had to stay alert to walk in Louisiana. Insects and pests loved the steamy climate. Rats ran along the rooftops and roaches—the size of hummingbirds—swooped about. Vicious humidity, scalding sun, raging wind and fierce thunderstorms erupted out of nowhere, exploding down the street and bringing swarms of mosquitoes. How dreadful that parts of this beautiful city were below sea level and the slightest rain flooded the drainage ditches. A sudden downpour could drench Kate's boots and petticoats and blow her off balance as she navigated the narrow streets. Kate couldn't flag a cab, and if it poured, she would have to duck inside a shop or hike up her skirt and run.

Kate looked past the magnolia and banana trees flailing their wounded limbs in the wind. New Orleans was actively rebuilding in the 1870s. In the face of all unknowns, some said it was a hopeful time for progressivism.[5]

TENSION RISING

Kate kept her delicate finger poised on the pulse of the thrumming city. But we wonder: When did she notice that all was not well? Political unrest was simmering. Did she ever fear for her safety? Kate likely avoided dangerous areas, steered clear of clumps of embittered men. Sometimes, extremist forays erupted because of the federal occupation. What did Kate make of it? In her writing and in her life, Kate avoided politics. Did she sense tension?

Did she worry about her hungry newborn at home with the nurse fuming? Babies nursed every two to four hours, sometimes every hour. How often

Top: French Quarter gutter and
street, New Orleans (1884–85).
*Photograph by Edward Wilson. The
Historic New Orleans Collection.*

Bottom: Pirates Alley, New Orleans.
Photograph by Rachelle O'Brien.

might change depending on the time of day, but no doubt it was eight to twelve times in twenty-four hours. Whenever she heard an infant scream, she tensed up. Her engorged breasts pained her. Mon Dieu, was she leaking through her dress?

Hopefully, little Jean was being rocked or was napping in the rockabye basket. Kate hoped it wasn't too exhausting frustrating for the nurse to distract him, jiggle him a while longer till Kate could breastfeed when she got back. Did Oscar mind that Kate was spending more time outside of the home?

But some God-force compelled Kate: *You must keep learning and seeing.* Smoking her Cuban cigarettes released her joy, increasing her walk-dependence for growth. Like Aristotle, Kate walked and fell deep in thought during meanderings around New Orleans.

Walking and observing, Kate saw how New Orleanians were always drawing loved ones close to protect each other. But she was not one of them. Could she ever be?

Chapter 4

DEGAS IS HERE!

ARRIVAL OF EDGAR DEGAS

1872

Into the web of infants screaming for milk, desperate husbands getting angrier and Kate sneaking off for walks, a genius showed up.[6]

The talented, mysterious Edgar Degas made his entrance in New Orleans in October 1872, the same year the Carnival Krewe Rex was founded. Oscar was distracted. Kate was intrigued. Edgar landed, carrying Carnival costumes from the Paris Opera and looking for people speaking impeccable French.[7]

As newly arrived outsiders and creatives in New Orleans, Edgar and Kate had a lot in common. They were both disciplined: Kate a talented pianist and Edgar a brilliant painter. Edgar traveled in the same Creole social circles as Kate and Oscar. He attended the same soireés, performances and limited operas.

The music scene lagged in comparison to Paris, and Edgar may have complained to them. Edgar wrote in one of his letters from New Orleans:

> *The absence of the opera has been causing me real pain....Instead, we have a troupe performing comedy, drama, vaudeville, etc., which includes numerous and rather talented actors from Montmartre.*[8]

When he arrived, Edgar spoke very little English, other than the two words he kept repeating: *turkey buzzard.* Creole Francophiles, like Kate and Oscar, spoke perfect French. Creole women enamored Edgar. He wrote:

> *The women are pretty and exceptionally graceful....Creole women have something captivating.*

If Kate and Edgar met, they may have talked of the Franco-Prussian War, in which he fought and the couple had been trapped.

No doubt disquiet ruled the Degas rental house, where Edgar was staying, jammed as it was with eighteen floundering relatives. Maybe he took breaks from painting his female relatives in their indoor worlds. Staying with his brother, his uncle and their extended families on Esplanade Avenue was indeed challenging for a bachelor. Edgar strolled around the city, past the fairgrounds on Esplanade Avenue, shielding his failing eyes from the fierce sun.

Edgar Degas in His Early Days, Joseph Tourtin (1860). *Albumen print from a collodion glass negative, in business card format. Gift of Alberto Martinez through the Society of Friends of the Musée d'Orsay, 1992.* © *Musée d'Orsay, Dist. RMN-Grand Palais / Alexis Brandt.*

Kate's and Edgar's family members worked literally next door to each other. Oscar had moved his cotton brokerage to the elite area on Carondelet Street, and the Degas brothers worked down the block as cotton merchants. Did they commiserate with each other?[9]

While Edgar was visiting (1872–73), many cotton brokerages, including the Degas family's, were about to collapse. Men grunted into their coffee, skipped the business section of the paper, welcomed any hopeful remark.

Uninformed wives often felt the tension in their husbands and grieved. They dared not speak as their spouses stuffed down dinner, occasionally so exhausted that crumbs dislodged from their mouths and clung to their lips. Sometimes these failing cotton broker husbands glanced down at a newspaper, then twisted it into a knot so their wives couldn't read it: a business closing, a building condemned, the obituary of a friend. Other times, they smiled benignly at their wives and shuffled off.

The Song Rehearsal, Edgar Degas (1872–73). Pianos were centrally located in many New Orleans houses, like this home. Kate Chopin resided nearby and enjoyed playing songs on her piano. Later, in 1888, H. Rollman and Sons published a song that Kate composed, called "Lilia Polka." © *Dumbarton Oaks, House Collection, Washington, D.C.*

Woman Seated on a Balcony, Edgar Degas (1872). In this painting, Degas depicted his Creole cousin on the balcony. The featured woman is either Estelle Musson Degas or Mathilde Musson Bell. Kate Chopin's Garden District home also had a balcony. Dr. Marilyn Brown described New Orleans Creole women on their balconies, which were both public and private spheres. *Ordrupgaardsamlingen Museum.*

Children on a Doorstep, Edgar Degas (1872). New Orleans houses in the Garden District were frequently surrounded by gardens and had shared courtyards. Houses often had high ceilings and large windows, as depicted here. *Ordrupgaardsamlingen Museum.*

Top: *Portrait of Estelle Musson De Gas*, Edgar Degas (1872). This cherished painting is the only artwork Degas created in New Orleans that found a permanent home in New Orleans. *New Orleans Museum of Art.*

Bottom: This photograph of Edgar Degas was taken shortly after he arrived in New Orleans (1872). *Louisiana Research Collection, Tulane University Libraries.*

Degas family tree. The author created this photo collage when studying the Degas family photograph archives at the D'Orsay Museum. *Photograph by Rory O'Neill Schmitt, PhD.*

The Cotton Office, Edgar Degas (1873). Degas depicted his brothers, his uncle and their associates at their family cotton office in New Orleans. Oscar Chopin worked nearby as a cotton factor. Some descendants of Kate Chopin reported that one of the figures possesses the likeness of Oscar Chopin. *Musée des Beaux-Arts, Pau, France.*

A traveler, not yet world famous but on the cusp of notoriety, was here. Degas was here: a wonderful celebration and distraction. Degas was known, after all, and he was here.

Edgar, whose late mother was from New Orleans, and Oscar, whose father was from France, were both trying to save their families in the cotton business. The men, years apart, were both ill equipped. What could an inexperienced banker or an artist do to fix the cotton situation? (We will see what happened at Carnival.) Edgar painted *A Cotton Office*, depicting his top-hatted uncle, his brothers and their eleven business associates idling in their soon-to-be-bankrupt office. Did Edgar paint Oscar? Descendants of Oscar recognize him in that masterpiece.

IT'S CARNIVAL TIME

1873

All were drowning in the cotton well of no sales and shame. Men eagerly looked forward to a respite at Mardi Gras when maskers in the Carnival krewes could parade the streets and release their rage and frustration in recreation. Locals lived for it, and some would even die in it.

Like all newcomers, Kate and Edgar were anticipating the famous Carnival, with its masquerade balls and parades. No longer postpartum, pregnant or in mourning, unrestricted from socializing, Kate could celebrate on the ballroom dance floor in a royal gown of purple, green, gold or the color of her choice.

But a horror lay in wait for them all.

The men in Kate's and Edgar's families were members of the same all-White private clubs and Carnival krewes. Admittance into the highest echelons of society gave them automatic approval from other businessmen. In perilous times, when deals often depended on friendship, acceptance meant a lot. These elite private clubs, like Mystick Krewe of Comus, also had political motivations and racist positions. Inside, behind locked doors, angry merchants complained about their floundering wealth and strategized uprisings against the local government. Outside of these locked doors, naïve visitors and entertaining wives drank tea and chatted about the latest Creole novel—two worlds kept distinctly and purposefully apart. Secrets worked better that way.

Oscar and the men of Edgar's family likely participated in the guarded krewe meetings and insurrectionist plots to ridicule the federal leaders in 1873. The disenfranchised planters wanted to take control of the municipal government. Krewe members were safe at club meetings because all members harbored revenge. Members had been ruthlessly screened, and the all-male clubs mostly barred all local non-members. The Carnival clubs were small (Comus, Twelfth Night and Rex being the main ones) and, like Greek fraternities, sworn to silence (or death).

Under the gleeful patina of the soirées, contempt raged. Edgar and Kate witnessed New Orleans ripe with hostile White radicals and mean-spirited men releasing their fury. Krewe members vehemently opposed the occupation of Louisiana by Union forces and the rise to power of African Americans and their supporters. Members denounced the racially integrated government and began planning to use the Comus parade to instigate unrest and, if necessary, to charge on the police. What shameful affair would Kate and Edgar witness?

Back then, membership in New Orleans Carnival society also overlapped with that of the insurrectionary, racist White League. (Oscar and Edgar's brothers and uncle belonged to both.) Many Southerners who had fought in the Civil War the decade prior had learned how to acquire secret armed shipments from New York. They were willing to stage an uprising—and give up their lives, if need be—if they thought they could get some control back.

But Oscar hadn't fought in the Civil War. No doubt he felt sheepish that he'd escaped Louisiana and found refuge in France. To mix with the privileged, he couldn't be known as an expatriate who hid in the French countryside.

How could Oscar have even been associated with the White League? Hadn't he fought his cruel father when he tortured enslaved laborers? Hadn't he even fled his brutal father with his mother?

How much of the insurrectionist plans did Edgar and Kate even know about? He was a foreigner, she a woman.

These members-only clubs restricted invitations to carefully evaluated and known male members, although they permitted some prestigious European guests. Was Edgar prominent enough and sought-after enough to go to the elite gentlemen's clubs? Though his uncle was planning to lead one insurrection, he may have excluded Edgar.

Back then, wives, like Kate, were treated like children: kept in a playroom or apart, so as not to upset them, and discouraged from going outside, where violence could break out at any time. We wonder if Kate noticed any peculiarities in Oscar's behavior. Questions likely raced through her mind. She probably found that when she inquired, answers weren't always forthcoming. Most Southern men shielded women from money woes by telling them: nothing.

Edgar and Kate probably didn't know about the underground bubble of ferocity of many cotton brokers, a bubble about to explode at a recreational activity on Mardi Gras day when least expected.

Mardi Gras: Rex by Day

Upper-class women, like Kate, watched parades not from the street but above the crowds. They were entertained on private verandas, club balconies and the front lawns of galleried mansions on St. Charles Avenue. Scurrying after little boys in white suits and girls in dresses with bows, they snatched mint juleps or Sazeracs from passing trays.

Wives waved at the floats or the stallions their masked husbands were riding and called out their names. The most powerful krewe members, who were lieutenants in the organization, rode stallions alongside the floats, whistling and ordering commands.

The Rex procession surged down St. Charles Avenue on February 25, 1873. Crowds gathered, awaiting the arrival of the king of Carnival at City Hall downtown. But the insolent king performed a mock arrest, seizing not only the mayor but also the former militia colonel and mortifying the police superintendent. The parade continued in a jocular fashion, as though it was all tongue in cheek. It was tongue in whose cheek? The Carnival clubs had disguised subversive commentary on the government as play. Were humiliated men, like Oscar and the Degas brothers, proud they had used merriment to undermine authorities?[10]

Mardi Gras: Comus by Night

The pageantry of the nighttime Comus parade in 1873 was even more sinister. At nine o'clock on the night of Shrove Tuesday, flambeaux carriers emerged from the darkness. They preceded a krewe of one hundred men, masked and dressed in elaborate insect costumes, riding atop mule-drawn floats. The public masquerade lampooned the Republican regime evoking Darwin's theory of natural selection.

St. Roch Cemetery entrance. *Photograph by Robert A. Schaefer Jr.*

The krewe members marched in papier-mâché insect costumes with huge animal heads. Edgar naïvely dressed in his elaborate Parisian insect costume. (By dressing as an insect that Carnival, did he realize he was aligning himself with radical, violent subversives?)

The floats were acerbic, naming politicians as hyenas and apes. The Metropolitan Police refused to clear pedestrian traffic for the insulting procession. But the maskers tried to push through the streets to end their procession at the fashionable Varieties Theater in the Faubourg St. Mary. Here, behind the locked doors, secluded wives waited in their long gowns, elbow-length gloves and silk shoes for a ball. Unsuspecting ladies were waiting until the stroke of midnight, when the festive assembly would dance, eat and drink until daybreak with their partners. (Children, who had probably gone to the daytime Rex parade, would be in bed and protected by family members.)

But before the krewe arrived at the theater, a chaotic outbreak of these masked insects erupted in the street. Oscar, Edgar's brothers and uncle and their colleague, Fred Ogden, led some of the violence that ensued. The krewe incited a mob to attack the Metropolitan Police. The lawlessness, no doubt, terrified everyone.

When did Kate and Edgar realize that their family members were associates of the anti-government, racist, insurrectionary group? How could Edgar have condoned inequality? Didn't he feel compassion for people of color? His White uncle had married a free woman of color, and he had both Black and White relatives. Wouldn't Kate practice compassion for all, being raised by Sacred Heart nuns, who taught her that love is integral to life?

THE FIRST BATTLE OF THE CABILDO

The violence didn't stop after the parades ended. This insurrection became a warmup for bigger and better-planned efforts to come.

The following month, Oscar and other Carnival club men, along with members of the White League, attacked the Cabildo in downtown New Orleans. Armed White supremacists attempted to seize the police station at Jackson Square. Over sixty people were arrested, and an innocent bystander was killed.

Edgar quickly exited Louisiana. He left for Paris, no doubt disturbed by the rioting that his relatives were spearheading and by the news of his father's financial collapse.

But Kate couldn't leave, even if she didn't approve of the violent insurrection. Wives, at that time, couldn't travel without a written letter of permission from their husband. She was trapped in a woman's body in a town where White male traditions were sovereign.

ST. LOUIS SAFETY

1874

Soon, Kate realized that she was pregnant again (as of December 1874). Did Oscar write her a permission slip, allow her to slip away to St. Louis, where it was safer and the climate more temperate?

Kate's doting mother, forty-five, and her grandma, sixty-three, couldn't wait to welcome Kate home that summer. She brought hope for Kate's married Aunt "Puss" and husband, who had buried two infants, and amusement for her other aunt and uncle, whose three children probably couldn't wait to hold the baby.

And Kate brought joy for her brother, Tom, who had reappeared after no one had seen him for a year or more. Soon, as proud godfather, Tom would be given a new chance to adore the little two-year-old. Then, too, Kate's doctor, Dr. Frederick Kolbenheyer, advised and encouraged her. Radical and brave (he'd been exiled from Austria), he would later mentor Kate throughout her life.

Dare Kate get used to this temporary safe environment in St. Louis? Her trusting family doctor, her fun-loving brother, her wealthy, caring mother, friends and relatives just a few steps away. Yes, oh my yes.

Six months after Edgar Degas left New Orleans, Kate survived the *accouchement* of her second son. Oscar Charles Chopin was born on September 24, 1873, and would one day become an accomplished visual artist. Kate was ecstatic.

But peril was fast on the heels of pleasure. It wasn't long before Kate's gratitude devolved into grieving. Two days after Christmas, Tom, her only surviving sibling, was dead.

Chapter 5

BRIDGE, BATTLE, BIRTH

FILLE UNIQUE (ONLY CHILD)

1874

A reckless buggy accident had killed Tom Jr. Death from plagues, disease and childbirth were expected, but death by accident was still a shock.

Horses caused most accidents and injuries, and wild Tom provoked them. Why? Men hid so much from their sisters and mothers. Was he filled with rage at someone? Resentment for something? Arrogance at the unreliable horses and treacherous roads? Would Kate ever know?

The outrageous Tom had acted like he was immortal racing his buggy, and so he had died at twenty-five. He would not be protecting his mother, his sister or his godson.

The male relatives in Kate's life had vanished: all proud, all leaving to command a train, a battlefield, a yoke of horses. Determined to outrun injury, make a name for themselves, they had crashed into death: father, brothers, all. By twenty-three, Kate was the only child, was the heir apparent, the man/woman matriarch of the family.

Kate rang in the new year 1874 in deep mourning, feeling dizzy, nauseous, dazed, numb. She may not have believed that her brother's death was real. She may have felt nothing till the dreaded seamstress came to replace Kate's regular postpartum clothing with mourning attire. Her wardrobe and ornaments would tell the death story: broaches, lockets, armbands, jewelry woven from her dead brother's hair.

Kate succumbed to the transformation, hoping it would distance busybodies; that over time, she would feel different emotions; that her brother had a quick death—no pain. Still, a hollow feeling seized her, grabbed her stomach: tightness or heaviness, in her chest and throat, oversensitivity to noise. This was her third major death (father and two brothers). Did she feel like life was closing in around her? Was she exhausted from trying to hold it together for two small children?

Nighttime was probably her most challenging time. Darkness tends to lower one's mood and usher in feelings of anxiety and despair. But during the night, her loving Oscar was there. Would he go the distance to hold her in her grief? Having buried his parents, Oscar knew about the irrationality of death, that it might take months and months to grieve her brother, that death would be staring in her face for a time.

Married four years now, Oscar and Kate might have grown closer with each birth and death if the cotton business hadn't anxietized Oscar and a third pregnancy hadn't unnerved Kate.

Kate was probably living in a state of catlike readiness for the next bad thing to happen, so she could be better equipped to process grief herself and cushion the blow for her mother or her husband. Did she fear her newborn or she herself would die in childbirth? Had Kate's luck finally run out?

Some say the only cure for grief is action. Did Oscar try to pull Kate from her heartache with their new, larger house on Constantinople Street in New Orleans late that summer in 1874? Or with a trip back to St. Louis to revive her spirit? She happily accepted both offers, perhaps not knowing by lifting her spirits, she was sinking their finances.

Travel was expensive, but oh, a trip with her husband would bring stories to tell and new things to see. The Fourth of July heralded the opening of the Eads Bridge in St. Louis, and she and Oscar would be among the celebratory group.

We imagine Kate smiled and waved while hundreds of neighbors stood in the sun and fresh air and cheered. She was there to witness joy and distract her family from the intense sorrow, pain and rumination over her brother.

But did she choke back tears recalling her father's bridge collapse? No matter what trauma she'd endured, Kate would bravely face up to the challenge.

Going into her mother's house, Kate likely saw her brother in everything. Did she help Eliza move Tom's mementos upstairs? See what purpose she could serve? Her mother's life, as Kate knew it and loved it, had been changed in ways she couldn't fully yet comprehend.

Kate Chopin resided near this house on the corner of Pitt and Constantinople Streets in New Orleans. *Photograph by Rachelle O'Brien.*

Maybe the most painful part of prolonged grief was having to mother her own mother alone, after Oscar returned to New Orleans for business. Tom's death was overwhelming to Eliza. No mother can ever be fully prepared for her adult child to die before her. Eliza had lost a twenty-five-year-old child—and friend. Everything Eliza had invested in Tom now seemed for naught, especially since he had died from a cause (reckless driving, reported in the newspaper) that made others uncomfortable or judgmental.

Keeping active was something Eliza could do with Kate. Life was happening around them and had changed in a way they didn't expect. But there were new joys, new opportunities, new faces to explore. Now Kate was there with her two baby boys, and with another babe coming, she'd no time for dark thoughts.

For a brief time that summer in St. Louis, Kate, twenty-four, wouldn't talk about Oscar's money woes, a political uprising or death carts clanking down the street in New Orleans. She would help her mother as a compassionate friend: allow her to tell the story of her loss, sit with her and be still and silent in her house without Tom Jr. Together, they might put the pieces together to help make sense of what had just happened.

But alone at night, in her childhood environment, after she'd put down her two boys, the pain no doubt welled up in Kate. Did she not drag out her journal, write as a way of coping to make sense of the pain? Kate hated seeing her mother so distraught, but in the evening by candlelight, she could relax and alter her mood with a pen and paper. She could write letters to Oscar and journal for herself.

Kate could muse on artistic things: painting, poetry, Degas. We wonder if she was beginning to sense her own mission to be an artist. Although she wrote long letters and kept a diary, she hadn't yet felt the stinging purpose to write professionally. Perhaps she hadn't seen enough suffering; maybe she had replaced creativity in suckling a child; but now sorrow was dead center in front of her, and she was probably writing about it.

BATTLE IN NEW ORLEANS

Oscar was even more destabilized than Kate's mother. He slinked back to New Orleans, leaving Kate and his sons behind. Secret military activities had magnetically pulled him home to battle again. Did Kate (now eight months pregnant) sense his unrest and fear if he was left by himself much longer, evil would occur?

Kate probably heard word of mouth about the upheavals in postwar New Orleans. Were more clashes afoot? Oscar had never been in a war—a real one, anyway. Not having served in the Civil War, he could easily feel pressured to prove his patriotism. But at times, did she fear him grabbing some rite of passage to become a Southerner? Would he use violence to stiffen his wounded ego and defy his draining bank account?

Oscar harbored a strange French attitude toward violence and was desparate to be above it. But he had become increasingly obsessed with it in Louisiana. He had been strapped and beaten by his barbaric father, and Kate thought she had pretty good idea of what Oscar was and was not capable of. But then, maybe she didn't. Maybe he had succumbed to the resentment of his colleagues in the floundering cotton business.

Had Oscar fallen into the resentment of the other men about him? Oscar and his friends, once Confederate soldiers, seethed in their rage. Oscar knew fighting was stupid, but now he had an instinctive desire to do it. We wonder if Oscar wrote to Kate that he had found his associates in cotton warming up for war, that he saw failure and fear looming behind the spiteful eyes of Mystick Krewe members.

Oscar had been in that parade street riot, but now a bigger attack was being planned. Did he feel, alongside these Southern brutes, that as a pacifist, he'd missed the branding necessary to become a man? Had the blood of his father and his ancestors instilled in him a tendency toward violence?

Or, was Oscar ashamed of the plans afoot? Did he write Kate that soon groups would unite for an attack, that it would be a carefully organized action, so they wouldn't repeat the mistakes of their unprepared mob of one hundred men at the Cabildo a few years back?

Fear reigned in New Orleans in 1874. Some said that there had been so much confusion and corruption in the prior year's governor elections that no one knew who had really won. Was John McEnery (Democrat) or William Kellogg (Republican) the winner?

Here's what happened, but we don't know how much Kate knew: bitter men, including Oscar, buckled down and prepared to fight. Near him, other struggling cotton factors, like Edgar Degas's brothers and uncle, fought because they believed they had to and yearned for more power, more money—by any means necessary.

On September 14, 1874, five thousand Louisianians congregated for a mass meeting at Royal and Canal Streets and demanded the resignation of Governor William Kellogg. The governor quickly fled to the nearby U.S. Customs House and put someone else in charge.

Then, Fred Ogden led 8,400 fuming White Leaguers in an attack on the New Orleans police and Black state militia. At the Battle of Liberty Place, White Leaguers pounded their coffers and severed the city's outgoing telegraph lines, constricting their hold on the city. They positioned snipers in buildings along the processional route, and the militia marched down Canal Street toward the integrated Metropolitan Police.

Guns fired. Oscar participated in the intense fighting that ensured, while thousands of onlookers watched. Some believed a turning point for Reconstruction had occurred.

Death seized the lives of sixteen White Leaguers, thirteen Metropolitans and six innocent bystanders. Within fifteen minutes, the Metropolitan Police retreated in defeat. And within hours, White Leaguers had overthrown the government. They controlled the city momentarily, before President Grant's army restored order.

No insurrectionist was ever prosecuted. Are we surprised? This act of omission would lead to further chaos and cruelty.

SEEING FOR HERSELF

Back in St. Louis, everything was confusing. Word of mouth was often inaccurate, and short of the newspapers (which often only had weekly editions), no reliable information prevailed. Kate likely read about the coup in the newspaper, horrified, mystified. Wobbling, pregnant, she probably searched for death notices. Was her husband even alive?

Kate steeled herself to hold on. Forty-four days after the battle, on October 28, 1874, she gave birth to George, whom she named after her Confederate soldier brother.

Shortly thereafter, twenty-four-year-old Kate traveled the six hundred miles with her newborn and sons, ages one and three, all the way home to New Orleans. She had to see for herself what was going on with Oscar, and the perils of nursing and changing three small babes and getting smallpox wouldn't stop her.

Kate likely knew smallpox was on the rise, killing one in three who contracted it in Louisiana. Did she ward off daymares of black vomit or blood shooting out of her children's eyes, noses and ears? Did she check her boys regularly for signs of yellow fever, which was also looming? Oh, if only that summer they could escape New Orleans for Grand Isle. Here, they could inhale fresh air, take parasoled walks on the beach, sink their toes into the warm sand. Kate was too encumbered now with toddlers to claim the serenity for which her soul ached.

Back in New Orleans, we wonder if Kate found Oscar increasingly distant, withdrawing to commiserate with his failing friends. He endured pressure-filled days as a cotton factor and wasted away at the club, puffing cigars and blithering resentment against the Reconstruction government.

In smoke-filled libraries full to the brim with regrets, his colleagues discussed propertied bankruptcy. Some mindlessly barged through doors; others, red-eyed with grief, conferred in private, hushed conversations, fearing a dissolution of their companies like that of the Degas Bros. one year prior.

The defeat of the Metropolitan Police hadn't put money in Oscar's dwindling bank account.

And, when Kate expressed her concern, did Oscar's friends gaslight her with platitudes? *But you have so much more than most women. Many women can't even read. Shouldn't you be grateful at least to have the skill to reread your Bible? Your babies haven't died. You keep giving birth to even stronger sons. Your mother always helps you.* (The fact that death had not taken its toll on Kate's babies was supposed to be a consolation.)

Left: *The Sick Room*, Edgar Degas (1872–73). In the 1870s in New Orleans, illness was so frequent that a room was often designated as a sickroom in the house, in order to shield the spread of infection to children and adults in the family. *Private collection, courtesy of Walter Feilchenfeldt.*

Below: Pitot House, exterior. The Pitot House is located in New Orleans's oldest European settlement area on Bayou St. John. The house was built in 1799 and is located at 1440 Moss Street. *Photograph by Rachelle O'Brien.*

OSCAR CHOPIN,

COTTON FACTOR

—and—

COMMISSION MERCHANT,

New Orleans.

———

NOTICE!

I HAVE ON HAND SEVERAL thousand pounds of "Paris Green," manufactured in St. Louis under my own directions, which I will furnish to Planters desiring it, in required quantities and at the lowest market prices.

To parties pledging their consignments of Cotton to me this Fall, I will "advance" the Paris Green with the flour or sprinkler necessary to apply it.

2t.   OSCAR CHOPIN.

Advertisement for Oscar Chopin, cotton factor and commission merchant, New Orleans, in the *Louisiana Democrat* (Alexandria, LA), July 11, 1877. Oscar promises advances or loans to customers.

Oscar had been struggling alone for a while, and under the influence of outraged men, he was probably gloomier. Amid economic collapse, political uprising and disease, men were challenging each other to duels for even the slightest trivial insults. (More duels were fought in New Orleans than in any other American city.) Did Kate fear Oscar would be challenged to a duel? At City Park, men fought with pistol, saber, bowie knife, sword and even poison pills.

Indoors at home, Southern men (even kind, thoughtful and admiring ones) tried to genuinely provide for, while simultaneously controlling, women. Now, Oscar had no new prospects to be charmed, no more cotton to be sold, no more rental houses to be relocate to. What was he to do? How could he give Kate the glamorous life he'd promised her in New Orleans? Some men had given up hope, hanging themselves from the Suicide Oak in City Park.

The Etienne de Boré Oak, known as the Tree of Life, Audubon Park, New Orleans. *Pen drawing by Billy Harris.*

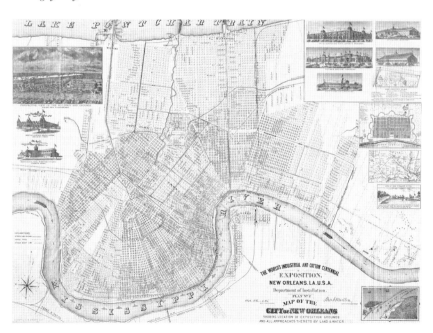

New Orleans Map, 1884. *Harvard Map Collection.*

Cotton Merchants in New Orleans, 1873, Edgar Degas. Since 1866, Edgar Degas's brothers had been running an import-export business in New Orleans, trading iron rails, cotton and wine. This painting, along with *The Cotton Office*, was featured in the 2023 Manet-Degas exhibition at the D'Orsay Museum in Paris and the Metropolitan Museum of Art in New York. *Harvard Art Museums/Fogg Museum, Gift of Herbert N. Straus, Photo © President and Fellows of Harvard College, 1929.90.*

Kate fierced herself to understand what exactly was going on with Oscar. Finding him stricken with overwork and exhaustion, beaten down by the woes of a disintegrating lifestyle, she visited the cotton warehouses. Kate described in her New Orleans journals how she caught on to cotton's decline and saw

> *pickeries, where damaged cotton was bleached and otherwise repaired. The whole process of weighing, sampling, storing, compressing, boring to detect fraud, and the treatment of damaged bales open to public view.*

She heard the rancor, the inconsolable wails—"Too much rain for cotton"— and the workers' caterwauling: "Cotton is shedding."

THE LASSO OF MOTHERHOOD

But her legs began to swell when baby George was just five months old. She felt bloated. Oh no, she couldn't be—but yes, she was. Kate was pregnant again.

Kate looked around New Orleans and prayed she had the strength to find some medical support here in 1875. She couldn't leave Oscar now. Not when he was so tired, sad-looking and blisteringly angry, not when he was probably too exhausted and humiliated to shuffle home before sunset. Death and more death loitered everywhere.

Sometimes, when she felt strong enough, Kate forged herself to walk to her husband's office. Other times, she waddled a few blocks to peer at the monstrous homes on St. Charles Avenue (as if looking up could inspire her). She was too large with child to hike far. Perhaps she shaded herself under the giant mama oak trees with moss drifting eerily over the sidewalk, hoping to spread wide their limbs over the brokenhearted.

She approached her second trimester, breastfeeding, bathing and changing babes in the brutally humid deep South. Kate birthed her fourth son, Frederick

Kate Chopin with her sons, Jean (b. 1871), Oscar (b. 1873), George (b. 1874) and Frederick (b. 1876), 1870–79. *Missouri Historical Society.*

New Orleans cemetery. *Photograph by Rachelle O'Brien.*

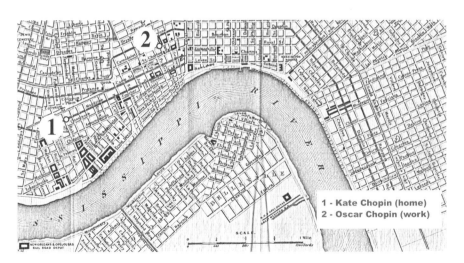

1 - Kate Chopin (home)
2 - Oscar Chopin (work)

Map of New Orleans with positions of Kate's house and Oscar's cotton office. *Provided by David Becnel.*

This historic Garden District home was built in the Second Empire style in 1872. This building has been part of the Louise S. McGehee School campus since 1929. *Photograph by Cheryl Gerber.*

Kate Chopin's home at 1413 Louisiana Avenue. *Photograph by Rachelle O'Brien.*

Above: This nineteenth-century double cottage on Esplanade Avenue may have served as an inspiration for Kate Chopin's setting of *The Awakening*. With special thanks to Dr. Tom Bonner and Dr. Bernie Koloski for their discovery. For more information, refer to Koloski's *The Historian's Awakening: Reading Kate Chopin's Classic Novel as Social and Cultural History* (2019). *Photograph provided by permission of Ashton's Bed and Breakfast, New Orleans.*

Left: Oscar Chopin with his son Jean Chopin. *Missouri Historical Society.*

(named after her doctor), on January 26, 1876. Soon after, she moved into a bigger rental home on Louisiana Avenue, framed by extensive gardens with weeping oak trees.

And still lassoed by motherhood, twenty-seven-year-old Kate became pregnant again and gave birth to her fifth son, Felix, in New Orleans in 1878. No doubt they couldn't relocate now, burdened as they were with children and belongings. But Oscar (who continually tried to uplift Kate with his boyish gestures of extravagance) impressed and soon fooled her when he moved to an even bigger office space at 77 Carondelet Street. Was Kate ignorant of the huge cotton yield loss in 1878 and 1879 and its impact on their depleting resources? We doubt it. Was she aware of how many cotton offices were empty and up for rent because of bankruptcies? Probably.

HONEY, I'VE SOME BAD NEWS

1879

Eventually, Oscar's bubble burst. He sat Kate down and disclosed the devastating news in 1879.

How did thirty-five-year-old Oscar tell Kate, pregnant for a sixth time? We imagine he shuffled home, walked zombie-like past his five wee boys and collapsed into Kate's arms. Maybe Kate reassured the children: *Papa's fine. No need to worry.*

In Oscar's sorrowful surrender, he finally revealed he was bankrupt. He couldn't pay off his debts or the rent for their duplex on Louisiana Avenue. Twenty-nine-year-old Kate probably wanted to bring her sharp brain to the task of helping. She'd watched her widowed mother run the household, manage properties and balance accounts. She'd seen the Sacred Heart nuns resolve issues.

Would Oscar indulge her, embrace her ideas or even hear her out? All of Kate's dowry had gone to him. Indeed, she was his possession. But would he listen to her?

Kate braced herself for the next debacle: a move to rural Louisiana, near Oscar's brother. Only he would take them in.

It was a bayou town called Cloutierville. Sneeze and you'd miss it.

Chapter 6

CLOOCHY-WHAT? HOW DO YOU EVEN PRONOUNCE IT?

Exit to the Bayou

1879

But Cloutierville? Had she heard right?

Did Kate tell herself the move was temporary? Perhaps the folks there could charm her for a few months.

But Cloutierville, really? A French parish of one hundred people in middle-of-nowhere Louisiana. Twenty miles from the nearest town, Natchitoches.[11]

How do you even pronounce "Cloutierville"?

But like most transplants, she was downright scared of what would follow. Would Oscar pay his debts in court? Or would medical expenses, loan payments, taxes pursue them? Perhaps Oscar could gain release from the shame of financial ruin, start again surrounded by his extended family.

Kate probably prayed that her life might just get better. But this last resort felt like a death blow.

Oscar's younger brother, Lamy, ran and owned the four thousand acres of isolated farms for cotton growing that comprised the Chopin lands. He had offered to let Oscar manage several small farms and the family general store. Would he be generous? Would he be cruel?

Hadn't Lamy recently wed a young socialite in January? Would she even want poor relatives nearby? Ah, the irony! Oscar had failed in New

Honey Island Swamp, St. Tammany Parish, Louisiana. *Pen drawing by Billy Harris.*

Orleans, but Lamy had succeeded in nowhere Louisiana. He had revived the family holdings, made improvements and presided over a beautiful mansion—all this by age twenty-nine.

SETTLING DOWN, SETTLING IN

Kate and Oscar squeezed inside his grandmother's house, which he'd (thankfully) purchased a few years prior. The old two-story house was clamped together with handmade square nails and stared out from the end of a dirt road. Downstairs served as storage, the second floor as living quarters. The kitchen, with its gigantic fireplace, was outside to protect from fires, which killed the unsuspecting. A hoop skirt, a child's sleeve, a toy mistakenly tossed could ignite a blaze that no mule-drawn fire carts could put out.

Pregnant Kate heaved up and down the outdoor steps all day. We imagine her feisty boys (ages eight, six, five, three and one) slid up and down the bannisters, leapfrogged or hid under wooden steps. How would she cram all five children into one bedroom and also make do with their small primary bedroom as the entertainment area and nursery?

Then, on December 31, 1879, God delivered a new hope. Kate gave birth to Lélia, her sixth child and her first girl.

Left: Kate and Oscar's house in Cloutierville, Louisiana, front view. *Library of Congress.*

Right: Water pump at Kate and Oscar's house in Cloutierville, Louisiana. *Library of Congress.*

BAYOU LEISURE

1880–82

At first, the bored villagers rallied for Kate and Oscar. Her first biographer explained:

In Cloutierville, Kate Chopin's home became the center of social life. Her inherited esprit or gaiety, that is, a sub-gaiety which was never frivolity, made her the delight of all her acquaintances.

Intellectually superior to her social equals who affectionately admired and approved her tact, her musical and conversational talents, and her astonishing gift of mimicry, she was, in the words of her daughter, the "Lady Bountiful of the neighborhood, dispensing advice and counsel, medicines, and, when necessary, food to the simple people around her, and in this way learning to know them and to love them too, for no matter how keenly they appealed to her wonderful sense of humor, she always touched on their weaknesses fondly and tolerantly, never unkindly."[12]

Kate Chopin enjoyed riding horses bareback while living on the bayou. Here, she is featured wearing fashionable riding garments and a riding hat (1870–79). *Missouri Historical Society.*

At first, country folk dismissed her daring as Kate discovered new life on the Cane River. She began to ride bareback. Morning, noon and night, they could see her in the fields.

BOSS GIRL

But then the gossips got uneasy, watching Kate run the general store, dressing glamorously and flirting with local farmers to get business, including a married roué named Albert.

Kate marched past those dreadful finger-pointing Christians with their pariah of a priest. So what if Kate defied the warnings of the Sacred Heart nuns who taught her, patrolling study hall, clicking their clackers, making girls sit up tall, legs together, ankles locked, skirts to the floor? What good were gold medals for intellect and deportment in this barren town, so closed in on itself that no one saw who she was?

But one rancher did. He looked proud, self-confident, well dressed, with a pointed, well-trimmed beard. He bragged about trudging home barefoot and bleeding from the siege at Vicksburg: a Civil War warrior, dashing, scandalous, irresistible. (We picture this horseman gambler like a cowboy, who wore a khaki jacket over unbuttoned blue denim shirt and jeans. He'd the kind of body that sunlight should expose.) But scandal followed him wherever he went. Though married, he had a reputation for being the best lover this side of the Mason-Dixon line. Women fantasized about a man who could leap on a horse, strip nude for a nap. Creole women forgot his sins for the balm of touch, for French whispers by moonlight, rumor said.

Albert Sampitié, Cloutierville, Louisiana. *From* Unveiling Kate Chopin *by Emily Toth.*

Wealthy and generous, the cowboy harnessed his French charm to woo Kate. When merchandise arrived for her store, by boat from New Orleans, she'd go down to the landing to get her goods and find him already there unloading them. He'd carry them back to the store, shelve them in an out-of-the-way back room, organize the invoices.

But Kate learned that he had developed his muscular, sometimes self-destructive, behavior through grit, pain and the trauma of war. Daytimes, he busied himself blind, charging his stallion over his endless land. Evenings, he socialized with a drink to calm his troubled mind, gambled and kept questionable company.

Kate heard whispers that he came from a line of proud womanizers and gamblers. Hadn't she heard that he beat his wife so much that she carried a black bullwhip? His French name literally meant "without pity." When he appeared on the horizon, a rush of feelings would arise in some ladies in town.[13]

Sometimes, the cowboy would "bump into Kate" when she was out in the fields. He liked to ride around the Cane River country, stripped to the waist, stallion sweaty, talking intimately with fellow landowners about boundaries and crops—and Kate liked to gallop bareback, skirts pinned up, hair free, smoking. His parcel of land adjoined hers, so it was not unseemly for him, if there were problems in the field, to meet up with Kate, even at night.

It must have been hard for Oscar. He was French, and Kate's flirtations, though fun and frivolous, fueled the gossips. The jealous had their eyes on Kate and whispered: *How dare she not milk a cow? How dare this lady from the city parade up and down the street in her fancy lavender clothes, show her ankles when strolling, go out alone, race bareback at night?*[14]

Wife-beating was French custom in Cloutierville, although not for Oscar. Local culture permitted beating scorned women. Rumor was, some nights on the bayou, vigilantes got drunk, lit their torches and went after women they despised. Publicly, Oscar defended her, but privately, maybe he requested: *Hold back, ma chère. S'il vous plaît?*

WE IMAGINE A SCENE in Kate and Oscar's life could have looked like this:

7:00 p.m. December 5, 1881. Cloutierville, Louisiana. A gallery of a mansion, which looks like the Pitot House on Bayou St. John in Mid-City, New Orleans.

                    KATE
   Discouraged, reading her words.
"One day, I'll pull myself together and determine what character of woman I am."

                    OSCAR
Why bother when I can tell you who you are.
   Laughs, sip from a glass.
You have grit. Shoot straight, ride tall in the saddle.
   He sits back in a chair, speaks slowly, with laid-back body language.

                    KATE
I won't join the long list of wives done in by their husbands. Close this general store,

diversify our crops, pay our debts. (*Holding up ledger.*) Good God. There are dozens of bills, going back…decades in this book. We've seven years of unpaid taxes. They're going to seize our land.

                    OSCAR
  Flustered.
All our overdue amounts are not even in that ledger. I don't even know where they are.

                    KATE
Find out.

  OSCAR looks right into her distinctly and intimately, swigs.

                    OSCAR
What I could show you slowly and thoroughly.

                    KATE
  Aroused.
What would you want in return?

                    OSCAR
To be the one man you can count on.
  Looks at her directly, quietly.
Don't you want your perspective to soften towards the world?
  Coughs.
How I've paced about—I allow you to walk alone, read, write, despite my exhaustion. Lord knows where you go, what you do and with whom. Smoking. Drinking.

                    KATE
Writing out here alone after dark. That's not radically wrong.

OSCAR

You swear nothing's wrong—when you write through the night. Tell that to the betrayed husbands who sleep alone.

KATE

It's the only time I have to write, Oscar.

OSCAR

Why do you do it? You don't need to. I provide for you. Pay your food. Your clothes. Your God knows what. I never question anything, though I should. Why do you write when it could hurt everybody?

KATE

I'm trying to perfect who I am at different stages. Writing helps me clarify—be a mother, sister, spouse to myself.

OSCAR grabs her journal, reads through it.

OSCAR

Spouse? There is nothing about me in this journal. It's consumed with some strange—
Quotes from the journal.
"The effrontery in Alcée's eyes drew all her awakening sensuousness." It's so humiliating. "Alcée took her hand and held it while he said his lingering goodnight." What if the children read this? Why write if it offends? When I see through your pages—the bleeding mosaics of your life—how little you value me. I haven't known everything I wanted. Just that I always wanted the best for you.

KATE

I know that.

OSCAR

I've been living in the confusion of others'
needs. For days, weeks, I put myself last, tried
to be decent, honest, compassionate whenever a
customer cried. And they cried all the time. I
hoped finally to get a business started. Late but
started. Plenty of retired cotton brokers run
general stores.
  *He stands, hesitates a minute as if in pain,
  stabilizes. The clock gongs. In the other room,
  they hear the sounds of kids crying out.*

OSCAR

I hope those God dang children don't scream
all night! What's happening to me? My brain is
shrinking, while my body expands.
  Burps, pounds chest.
I ate too much. Overindulged. But it's all I got!
  Coughs.

  Another scream.

OSCAR

To kids, rattled: Shush.
  To Kate: Kate. I don't want to lose our…silver
strand connection. You are the darling of my
life. After making love to you, I felt like I was
being cradled to sleep by God, wrapped up in a
warm luxurious blanket that shielded me from the
world. Major concerns could be waved away. All I
had to do was conjure up the two of us wrapped
naked together. The all-night blissful embrace.
Please. Don't write any more. It's distracting you
from the children, agonizing me and wrinkling your
beautiful face.

KATE

It's not that easy. Thoughts swarm in like
butterflies. I have to grab them or—

OSCAR
They are of imaginary importance, unsuitable for
anyone to read, flagrantly cruel at worst. Sorry,
but it's true. Sorry, lovey. Now come to bed
and let me cheer up your mouth, your neck, your
breasts.
   Exits.

   *Kate withdraws, disturbed and broken, goes
purposely to her journal and begins writing.*

ALL'S NOT WELL ON THE BAYOU

If Kate pestered Oscar to return to city life, he likely lent a deaf ear. She was urban, he was now committed rural. He had been born in that Cane River country, and there he would die.

But Oscar started to cough, grow weaker. He couldn't seem to shake this illness. Affection under such circumstances was nigh on impossible. For ten years, Oscar had indulged Kate, and she was pregnant more often than not. He had pleased her with intimacy, and many things were forgiven in the dark of night.

But now the doctor confirmed Oscar had malaria. Some suspected it was from the vicious mosquitos that infested the Acadia swamp. Kate placed crude petroleum in puddles to keep them from breeding. Inside, she stretched more and more mosquito netting around their bedroom. She prayed the mosquito bar they slept under would protect them.

Malaria, what locals called swamp fever, gripped Oscar tighter and tighter, strangling his energy.

Kate likely wanted to help him but not humiliate him by showing she noticed. Watching him from their balcony, did Kate cry seeing him limp down to their filthy feed store, of which he was no doubt ashamed? She begged his clerks to demand cash, not credit, at his shop. He'd already instructed them not to charge customers who seemed to be "deserving poor."

The rancher next door offered to help, using his business acumen when needed. Soon, he was managing the shop's invoices, collecting money at 8

Horse and buggy in rural Louisiana. *Photograph by George Mugnier. Louisiana State Museum.*

percent interest from Cloutierville residents, keeping the Chopins' invoices with his own personal papers, balancing their books, overseeing repairs, replenishing the pantry.

More townspeople sniggered. Hadn't Kate heard the rumors that this cowboy was a violent, angry man who gambled, drank too much, beat his wife? Envy loomed in the swampy Louisiana village, especially when the rich got richer, handsome men even handsomer. And neglected wives indulged.

Kate's concerned mother visited and stayed in a small back room upstairs. Did Eliza implore Kate to return to St. Louis? Did she urge Kate to go back to church and pray?

Oscar was stout, feverish, morose. The rancher neighbor was generous, muscular, silent. He knew Cane River farming and had survived and even made money off the Civil War. Kate began leaning on him. She wouldn't let herself see how much.

Oscar went to Hot Springs for a treatment alone; Kate escaped to St. Louis alone. Did she see her husband return with a bleaker personality? Was it frightening to witness his poor health, his weight gain, his angry

City Park Bridge, New Orleans. *Photograph by Rachelle O'Brien.*

disposition when helped? Did Kate fear that soon, only Oscar's ghost would remain? He was having a harder time climbing steps, pausing to catch his breath, recenter himself.

Kate likely paced on the porch, hoping Oscar would improve, her senses would calm and another infected mosquito wouldn't bite the children. Kate probably shielded them from the trauma of witnessing their father's demise.

93

City Park, New Orleans. *Photograph by Rachelle O'Brien.*

By October 1882, Oscar couldn't ride, run, stand boldly for any length of time. Headaches, nausea, chills and high fever took hold.

The country doctor stressed that the malaria would run its course. Dr. Sam Scruggs hadn't studied anywhere for forty years. Perhaps Kate worried he had misdiagnosed Oscar and Oscar had yellow fever, not malaria. The doc visited frequently in October and November, leaving with a perplexed, scared look. In December, he came almost daily, treating three of their children for illnesses and starting Oscar on quinine.

The doctor sent medicine through his gorgeous, blonde daughter-in-law. Educated in Cuba by nuns, she was just three years younger than Kate. She served their bayou community by tiptoeing in and out, delivering medicines and offering her help as a seamstress. Though married, she lived mostly apart from her husband. Some whispered she'd only married him to have access to his brother-in-law, the debonair rancher in town.

Then, Kate's five-year-old, Fred, got malaria. And, morbidly depressed, Oscar doubled the amount of quinine he took. Fred would rebound, but Oscar never did. Soon, life forever vanished from his once-cheery face.

Death Notice

1882

We learn with sorrow the death of Mr. Oscar Chopin, so well and favorably known in this parish. He died on the 10th in Natchitoches parish, aged 39 years. He had retired from the Cotton Factor's and Commission business, which he had pursued in New Orleans for many years and had established himself on his plantation in his native parish, when death called him away. None better than we can attest to the pure and noble, upright and manly spirit of the departed. We tender our condolence to the bereaved family.[15]

Chapter 7

BAYOU SECRETS, BAYOU PAIN

The Widow Kate

With Oscar's death, everything changed.

Thirty-two-year-old Kate embarked on heavy mourning, concealing her face with a crepe veil, wearing black garments for two and a half years. She had observed death preparations before, but now she was in charge.

Isolated and incomplete, Kate had lost a part of herself. Their home looked like a different place, odd and distanced. She steered clear of certain areas of the house that were too-painful reminders. Kate was likely missing what she had lost: not just her husband—he hadn't been that for a while—but the person who used to protect her.

The hours that followed Oscar's death were full of activity yet empty of life. Kate probably sleepwalked through things, so numb that she was often completely unaware of her surroundings.

Caring for the Corpse

In death, did Oscar's body appear smaller than life? The face was unnaturally pallid. Who would shave it, trim his moustache?

Oscar's body would have to be washed and prepared before the joints stiffened. She would have to find ice to cool the body? Was there even ice in this town? So many horrid details.

The Laura Plantation was built in 1805 and is located in Vacherie, Louisiana (about fifty-five miles from New Orleans). *Pen drawing by Billy Harris.*

Kate had to summon the strength to direct Oscar's wake, while praying for grace to console her distraught children. Her bedroom would become the throne of horror, where everyone worshipped over Oscar's body.

Who would help bereft Kate? The priest was ambivalent toward her, hadn't visited with the last sacraments because she had defied him, refusing to leave Oscar to catch and saddle up the priest's horse.

Creole custom called for Kate to sit by the casket for three days to ensure death had occurred. Would any mourners help her guard the casket—lest cats or dogs jump on it, gnaw the flesh?

Maybe the rancher dropped by, dismounted his gray stallion, offered his help. Perhaps he stopped the clock at the hour of Oscar's death, draped the mirrors and portraits in black crepe, hung a black wreath on the door.

◊ ◊ ◊

WE IMAGINE A PHANTOM scene in Kate's life could have looked like this:

December 1884, late afternoon in rundown house, Cloutierville, Louisiana.

The living room is draped in black: wilting funeral wreaths, shrouded mirrors, pictures and furniture. Kate Chopin sits alone. The rancher neighbor appears outside in the rain.

RANCHER

Kate! Kate!

KATE

You can't come in.
She hesitates, refusing to look at him, infect herself with anything he is about.
Oscar's barely cold.

RANCHER

Breaking in. He pushes his body toward her, so she has a clear view. Kate laughs nervously.
I follow my feet, and they directed me here. You can't lock yourself up.

KATE

I'm in hiding. I can't find eighty dollars to pay for the mortician.

RANCHER

Handing her money.
Done. You look rough.

KATE

I'm not in my right mind. I wake after three hours—creditors at the door—relatives grabbing—

RANCHER

Have you eaten anything?
He uncovers a basket filled with delicacies and daffodils.

I decided to play the Southern gentleman. Here's fresh bread, Bouillabaisse, champagne.

                    KATE

You're not staying.
  Kate removes a cigarette, he leans in quickly to light it for her.

                    RANCHER

It'll take a few months—for the shock to settle in.
  He lights up a smoke for himself.

                    KATE

You saw the obituary. A description is given of Oscar so you can experience him slightly alive. I wrote one, but they wouldn't use it.

                    RANCHER

Read it to me.
  He stands with his shoulders, chest, hips and feet all pointing in her direction. He holds her gaze for a bit longer than appropriate.

                    KATE

  She reads from her journal.
"A huge spirit flew to God today. Oscar Chopin, husband, father, uncle, cousin, friend. An adventurer always ready to travel to Paris, or Berlin, or Cologne. A sportsman who loved the outdoors and saw his children did so, too. And when he couldn't do sports, joyfully watched the sunrise and sunset from his balcony on Main Street. A road he had loved to cross as a child making his way down to the bayou, stick in hand. Oscar, we send your soul to God."
  Sobs.

                    RANCHER

I'll remove these wreaths—

He puts out her unfinished cigarette and she
immediately lights another.

                    KATE
Don't touch anything.

                  RANCHER
The flowers are wilting...
  He looks around, concerned.
They've taken the children?

                    KATE
Temporarily, maybe forever. Lamy claims I drove
Oscar to overdose.

                  RANCHER
You didn't kill Oscar. His relatives demanded
an extensive autopsy. Oscar had forty grains of
quinine in his bloodstream, four times the maximum
dosage prescribed. He left his power of attorney
to his brother, his body to science and his debts
to you.

                    KATE
  She reads from a copy of Oscar's will.
All our assets are mortgaged. We've $12,000 in
cash debt. Seven years' unpaid taxes.

                  RANCHER
Sit back. Breathe. Your mother's coming?

                    KATE
No.
  Voice breaking.
She can't travel—her health's too fragile.

                  RANCHER
I brought you daffodils. They're so yellow; when
you hold them, you see spring. And your lavender
lantern for strolling in the moonlight. Come here.

                    KATE
Let's get this straight. This is my body, not yours.

                   RANCHER
I'm obnoxious, I know. Afterward, you'll love it.

                    KATE
Don't touch me.

                   RANCHER
I understand your objections.

                    KATE
We didn't do—

                   RANCHER
Everyone believes we did.

                    KATE
We may need to leave Cloutierville…

                   RANCHER
I'll cut people out of my life before I cut
Louisiana. I own half the state…
  He peruses her diary.
May I?
  Kate nods.
  He reads slowly from The Awakening.
"She let her hand lie listlessly, as though her
thoughts were elsewhere. She sat once more upon
the sofa beside Alcée. He had not stirred. She
put her arms about his neck. 'Good-bye, my sweet
Alcée. Tell me good-bye.' He kissed her with a
degree of passion which had not before entered
into his caress and strained her to him."
  Alcée is me? Yes?

                    KATE
Yes.

IN MOURNING AND IN DEBT

A spouse's death plunged women into widowhood—a perilous state some might never leave. Kate didn't want to become one of those widows who were ostracized as outcasts. Brothers, husbands, fathers, in-laws might declare them insane. The highly sensitive were treated for hysteria and the outspoken unconventional ones, like Kate, permanently locked away.

Kate knew that a widow's possessions, land and even children, could be taken from her. She dealt with Oscar's personal effects with low physical energy and stamina, careful to not neutralize the house to maintain a presence of Oscar. This was Oscar's house, his village, part of the Chopinville estate. Her brother-in-law was fighting for custody of her children, ages eleven, eight, seven, five, four and two. Kate was fighting back.

Before, Oscar had protected her during difficult situations by behaving with apparent confidence. But now, Kate was alone in a remote Cajun village where cuckolded men sought revenge. And gossipmongers blabbered Kate was an adulteress. Would she be lassoed, strung up and hung from a tree as a pariah? Her tight-fitting riding habit of blue cloth ripped from her skin. Her orchid blouse and buff gloves yanked off. Her jockey hat flung to the ground, pretty boots with heels sailing into a tree.

Did Kate worry how long she could last in Cloutierville, much less send six children off to boarding school because school there ended in fourth grade?

Where would Kate even find books to read, people to talk to? The educated country priest hadn't even recorded Oscar's death in the church register.

Kate could deny the no-future smallness of the place—the one church, one cemetery, one tiny schoolroom place. She knew there was more to life than the two long rows of very old frame houses facing a dusty road, than Oscar's grandma's house crumbling away, than the stretch of lonely fields, forests, swamps.

SECRETS AND SCANDALS

But then this rich rancher, this charming cowboy, this Southern gentleman savior had smitten her. With him, did Kate feel safe? The man was athletic, generous, bigger than life. He had made enough money to invest in Colorado land, own three cotton farms and employ forty-two people.

He rode past her house, horse's hooves kicking dust, hat cocked back, bare chest moist with sweat: how could she not love the loudness, the boldness, the fierceness of him? The cuss-your-way-down-the-road of him. Out there in the middle-of-nowhere Louisiana, parched grass on each side of the one-road town, he was life, he was future, he was action.

When this rancher loitered about the general store, did Kate relax? There wasn't a person or a place he wouldn't confront on his stallion, with sweat dripping and hair flying. There wasn't a debt he couldn't find out how to erase.

So what if Kate had medical and funeral bills; debts for the store, livestock, vehicles; inheritance issues; and, years of taxes on French Quarter property and on Natchitoches land, including the family's own home? He could help her resolve anything. She would follow instructions, collecting money due her, holding a public auction of all the real and personal property, she could spare.

So what if shadowy women appeared out of nowhere, no doubt looking for him at the store—mute women peeking around a rear window or carrying daffodils? No doubt, the town seamstress was always sashaying in and out carrying a basket of clothing for him, offering to make alterations—free of charge.

Women would put up with a lot to keep a man like that. This cowboy was a strapping big man. Kate saw that his wife was a small, plain woman. She blended into the bleak, dusty landscape. He rode wild above it. For a time, his wife refused to divorce him. Did she forgive his duplicity? There are things men do in the softness of the night that fools a woman into believing they will be faithful again.

Locals gossiped. What went on when he visited the homestead of his wife, who was always sickly and weak? He had had six children by her, even if only two survived, all baptized Catholic. Did he have supper with the children, spend the night there, look at his wife with any warmth or only treat her cruelly?

LOVE, LUST AND LONGING ON THE BAYOU

Maybe Kate could thrive in rural Louisiana because she had a secret. Kate wrote that love sprang from animal instinct and was in a measure divine, irresistibly fed by an indefinable current of magnetism.

The statue *The Centaur Nessus Kidnapping Deianire* is in collection of the Louvre Museum, Paris. *Photograph by Nikki Holley.*

When Kate and the cowboy came together, magnetism ruled. Their country nights were filled with the droning and humming of insects and the croaking of frogs. Country nights were so much darker than they ever were in cities. Country nights were a time of quiet and mystery and wonder.

In the privacy of her own home (and her own bedroom), only Kate Chopin knew what whispers were spoken, secrets projected, pleasures fulfilled. How could she not have touched deep love, as her later writings burned with primal passion? Kate defied taboos describing a woman's breasts, a man's breathing, heart beating, the ferocity of the climax, writing:

> *When he touched her breasts, they gave themselves up in quivering ecstasy, inviting his lips. Her mouth was like a fountain of delight.*[16]

We know that Kate had a connection with this strapping Cloutierville man and gifted him an amethyst lantern and a gaming table. How deep? How long? Some believe her stories were inspired by him rather than Oscar. Kate wrote:

Alcée riding by comes in for shelter. A sudden thunderbolt sends her into his arms, and a wordless impulse propels them into the bedroom. Before, they had held back, but now—everything seems possible....

Her firm, elastic flesh that was knowing for the first time its birthright, was like a creamy lily that the sun invites to contribute its breath and perfume to the undying life of the world.[17]

Did they have a romantic relationship? No one could prove it. Some believe they had a probable "brief romantic attachment" after Oscar's death, from 1882 to 1884.[18] Rumors were that Kate stayed for a time with this man, and his wife knew. And his daughter reported that Kate destroyed her parents' marriage.

LOVING AND LEAVING KATE

Despite the fantasy, Kate would have to confront the reality that he was married. Even if Kate wanted to wed him, she could never do so. Louisiana civil law divorce laws for infidelity forbade the offender from marrying his accomplice. And divorce was off the table. (Everyone in the town was cradle-to-grave Catholic. Among Catholics, there was no divorce.)

But soon, Kate began to have misgivings. The rancher rode his horse recklessly, drank more than he should, kept more and more disreputable company, and had his eye on someone else.

A vixen with golden hair, with a broad-smiling mouth, tip-tilted nose and full figure. Three years younger than Kate, Maria was the town seamstress. She flaunted Spanish mantillas, and twisted pearls and flowers into her curly blonde hair. She lived in a house across the horse lot from him with her two children, and he was paying her bills.[19]

KATE'S GOODBYE

Kate's romantic relationship, like a small mustard seed, had kept sprouting until it exploded. Maybe their final goodbye went something like what follows:

Cloutierville, General store, closing time. The sun is setting.

Kate's neighbor, the rancher, restocks cans in the empty general store.

Kate approaches him from behind, wrap her arms around his waist, rests her head on his back, breathes him in.

                    KATE
Let's take a cottage on the Baltic Sea.

                    RANCHER
I can't—

                    KATE
Let's elope to Paris. I wouldn't take advantage—

                    RANCHER
You'd be the first woman who hasn't.

                    KATE
Let's tell the world we're a pair.

                    RANCHER
I can't—
  When I think of a genuine relationship, with a woman who accepts me, I shudder. I've thought this through, many a black night. Uncertainty may be what attracts you—

                    KATE
I like who I am when I'm with you.

                    RANCHER
That scares me. I need to be honest—

                    KATE
Can't this wait till—

RANCHER

What you like about me has a dark side. I can't marry you.

KATE

I never asked you to.

RANCHER

But you will, you should… For your children, at least. I stand before this huge cliff and I'm… going to Colorado.

KATE

Colorado? *(Pause.)* We'll go, too.

RANCHER

I need to see some land.

KATE

You can't leave now.

RANCHER

You're forbidding me?

KATE

I'm finally debt-free, but for how long?

RANCHER

I'll return.

KATE

Your dream is with me.

RANCHER

It was… Is.

KATE

Go on… leave!

RANCHER

Hit me. Hurt me if you want. You acted with dignity. You deserve better.

She ties back her hair.

KATE

I probably thought of you four times for every once you thought of me.

RANCHER

Not true.

KATE

People said you were a loner, fickle, violent.

RANCHER

Lies.

KATE

You don't get that reputation without some transgression.

RANCHER

I gave you my heart—at least to a point.

KATE

You want to get back on the carousel. Go. Find some younger, simpler woman. No intellect there.

RANCHER

Maria says you do fine alone.

KATE

What?

RANCHER

You and I can continue to grow. Just separately, for now. We can come back together at another time, dear.

KATE

The rumors are right. You're seeing—

RANCHER

It's just… Part of me loves you deeply, but a bigger part loves freedom more.

KATE

Whom will I count on?

RANCHER

Aren't you mostly happy with your own creative world?

KATE

You disgrace me with your ambivalence. Get out! I'm too strong for your world … where spinelessness triumphs.

RANCHER

You should go home to St. Louis—

KATE

You can't pass a cat without stroking it.

RANCHER

Get the anger out.

MARIA arrives at the door.

KATE

It's Maria isn't it? Oh my God. She drips magnetism. But she's got a lot of tiger in her, a lot of pitbull.

Grabs a bullwhip, cracks the floor. MARIA exits.

KATE

Go quick, leave. Get out. Before I stop you. Have pity and— Never come back. No matter how I cry. Or

beg. Don't… call again. Have mercy on me. Leave my
sight.

RANCHER
Calling back.
And what will you do?

KATE
Take a ride with God.

◇ ◇ ◇

BYE-BYE, BAYOU

Cloutierville had fulfilled every dread. For every night she'd cried, endured hardness, curled up in a ball and screamed, she hoped to heal in St. Louis. Kate rented out her farmhouse and escaped the bayou.

Widowed, she needed no approval papers to travel. Thirty-four-year-old Kate boarded a train, burdened with kids who were probably screaming and protesting, likely wanting to cling to the only house they knew. Louisiana was their forever home.

But Kate was going to her mama's to save herself.

Kate and Oscar's house in Cloutierville, Louisiana. *Library of Congress.*

Chapter 8

MISSOURI SHOCK

A St. Louis Daughter Returns

1884

Kate retrenched to St. Louis for the school year starting September 1884 with children ages four, six, eight, ten, eleven and thirteen. She would saddle up with those she loved and forget those she hated. After fourteen years in Louisiana, could she revive her old self, heal her wounds, yank off the shroud of grief?

Back then, widows carried the disgrace of the men who jilted, bankrupted or diminished them. But being married to a scoundrel was better than being the widow of a saint. Only the luckiest widows could bury their heartbreak in the homes of their rich mothers.

Kate beamed at the thought of her bountiful mother. Eliza's innate wisdom and calm would soothe Kate's shattered heart. Eliza would revel in the Sisyphean task of integrating her boisterous grandchildren into St. Louis society, where they would advance at top-notch schools.

But could St. Louis fill Kate's loneliness cup? Could Kate discard the chalice of pleasure she'd discovered in Louisiana? Would she evolve into a brainy woman, hands folded, voice cackling and breathless? Body straitjacketed? Could Kate trade the full woman she'd become for a sedate life as a Midwestern widow?

A Rude Awakening

1884–85

Shock met Kate at the front door. Dependent relatives had taken over Eliza's house; they blubbered about a trusted friend who had swindled Eliza's assets. Could distance and her own sorrow have blinded Kate to the catastrophe at home? Or had her mother withheld news, so as not to grieve Kate further?

Gray-haired and gaunt, Eliza rattled out, chest sagging, eyes distraught. Would Kate have to care for her aging mother, as well as her children? Kate moved her mother and children across the street to a rental house at 1122 St. Ange. But more tragedy struck.

Eliza got cancer, a fast-growing, inoperable kind. There was no way for Kate to save her. Loss toppled onto more loss.

On Sunday, June 28, 1885, at noon, with magnolias blooming outside, Eliza died.

All of Kate's hopes collapsed. Death does that.

Sunday had once been a joyous day for Kate. She'd married Oscar on a Sunday, and now, on a Sunday, her mother had died.

Kate accompanied her mother's casket into Holy Angels Church, watched it placed before the altar where she wed Oscar. She followed the casket to Calvary Cemetery, passed stone pillars, wee slabs on mounds of earth marking father (forty-nine), infant sisters, grandmas, brothers (age twenty-three and twenty-five).

At plot section 3, lot 9, Kate watched ushers use pulleys and ropes to lower her mother's coffin. Did Kate want to crawl in the casket with her mother near the graves of those whom she'd lost?

She had likely sobbed a bit before and during the ceremony. But the moment they lowered the casket, did Kate burst into a full emotional breakdown? Kate wasn't prepared for a final goodbye.

The world would drone on happily without Eliza, but could Kate? None of Kate's sorrows, joys or accomplishments mattered with her mother underground.

Gargoyle statues snarled as she left the cemetery. Kate had no fear left. Everything was likely stopped up inside her.

Kate likely told herself she would rise above what other women drown in. Still, mud slashed at her shoes as she slogged home, motherless, to her brood of fatherless children.

Oh, why oh why had she left Louisiana? Cloutierville was a bestial place, but she knew it—could work the store, could let her children be poorly educated but fed. Here, she was alone in brutal Missouri, and it would be freezing come winter.

A WRITER IS AWAKENED

1885

Kate's Austrian doctor studied her shriveling in her mourning clothes. Dr. Kolbenheyer, perhaps the smartest man Kate ever knew, remembered her well-written letters from Louisiana and urged her to seize a purpose for her life: to write.

Kate had these small, perplexed faces looking up at her. How could she make a change and create hope for their future?

Kate knew she needed a fresh environment, a place where she wouldn't have to be reminded about her past, her lost mother, her lost husband, her lost childhood. So she moved across town to a new home on Morgan Street, a place where she could revive the woman she wanted to be, become the one her children could admire and imitate, like she had her mother. Tragedy had never flattened her before, and at thirty-five, it wouldn't squash her now.

Kate would follow the doctor's orders, sculpt a new future, dredge up her skills in order to write and write well. No matter, Kate would lean in. She would use her talent to make a living and would excel, like Degas.

IMPRESSIONISTIC KATE

A remark in one of Edgar Degas's conversations troubled Kate until she wrote her novel *The Awakening.*

Edgar deeply respected exceptional sister-artists Berthe and Edma Morisot, who made their debut exhibiting one year before him at the Salon in Paris. But women, barred from state-sponsored art education in France, had to study art in expensive private studios. Few could race to the top with their male art counterparts.[20]

The Morisot sisters were fierce, determined, on fire. Their art instructor warned their mother that with intensive training, they would actually become painters. "Do you realize what this means?" he implored. "In the

Le Berceau by Berthe Morisot (1872). *Oil painting, purchased in 1930.* © *Musée d'Orsay, Dist. RMN-Grand Palais / Patrice Schmidt.*

upper-class milieu to which you belong, this will be revolutionary, I might say almost catastrophic."[21]

No matter; brave Maman Morisot, committed to her daughters achieving their potential, paid for them to continue training (with pupils of the masters Ingres and Delacroix, no less). A woman developing her talents was an act of revolution, self-actualization an act of defiance in the 1870s.

The Mother and Sister of the Artist, by Berthe Morisot (1869/1870). Edgar Degas is believed to have told Kate Chopin about the talented Morisot sister-artists. *National Gallery of Art Chester Dale Collection.*

Later, when thirty-year-old Edma Morisot married and became Edma Pontillon, she quit painting, surrendering to the life of a housewife in the French countryside. She later deeply regretted her decision in her letters to her younger sister.

Rather than being the creator, Edma became the object of others' gaze. Berthe immortalized her sister in her portraits: Edma filled with worry;

Portrait of Madame Edma Pontillon, née Edma Morisot, Sister of the Artist, Berthe Morisot (1871). *Pastel on paper, Legs Mme Pontillon, 1921© RMN-Grand Palais (Musée d'Orsay) / Hervé Lewandowski.*

Edma relieved, looking adoringly at her baby in a bassinet; Edma with her child in nature or resting on a chaise lounge.

When Berthe painted a portrait of her pregnant sister, dressed in black, perhaps she showed her fear of losing her. This portrait at least would capture her last days if the childbirth killed her. In this portrait, Edma's

Author Rory Schmitt studying Berthe Morisot's paintings at the Louvre Museum. *Photograph by Rachelle O'Brien.*

crinkled hands are well executed but in an awkward position. They look almost gnarled. Was Edma clenching in pain from a contraction? Were her hands reminding us of Edma's refusal to use her talented painter hands?

Edma was stuck, a prisoner in her home with her family. She could not freely leave, travel, have leisure at her will. Society wanted pregnant women home, protected, chained.

But Berthe defied expectations and pursued her passions, becoming one of the most famous founders of Impressionism, alongside Degas.

Did Edgar warn Kate of the dangers of women artists annihilating their talents? Did this news shake Kate into creating Edna's character in *The Awakening*, Edna Pontillier, who quits painting when she marries a Creole cotton factor? (Notice how Edma Pontillon and Edna Pontillier possess nearly identical names. Chopin scholars find it hard to believe this naming convention was accidental. Chopin was nothing but deeply purposeful.)

Did Edgar's revelation disturb Kate? Did Edgar's own sense of purpose ignite Kate?

Maybe Edgar gave Kate courage to keep writing and journaling, despite her fears. He himself painted eighteen hours a day.

Chapter 9

PHOENIX RISING

But the beginning of things, of a world especially, is necessarily vague, tangled, chaotic, and exceedingly disturbing. How few of us ever emerge from such beginning! How many souls perish in its tumult![22]
—*Kate Chopin*

WRITING AS A WAY OF KNOWING

Kate entered the mess of writing to heal, to learn and to make a living. When confusion took hold, she may have reminded herself that writing was what the doctor had ordered. Kate wouldn't allow herself to collapse in Midwestern regret.[23]

When feeling so lonely that she felt her brain would explode, Kate wrote. We envision her back at 3317 Morgan Street, where she sat down, grabbed her head as if frightened, pulled out a notebook and began to write. She couldn't seem to relax, quench the anxiety; she coughed, dipped her pen in ink.

And when she did, she wrote about Louisiana. Did writing allow her to forestall fright and revisit hauntings of her past? Many numb themselves to agonizing experiences, but Kate reexperienced them to better understand.

Some writers get cursed, some birthed as they reconnect. Kate commanded her trembling hand to write out those impressions of Louisiana. And the deeper into Louisiana she got, the more obsessed with

Left: Kate Chopin residence at 3317 Delmar Boulevard in St. Louis. *Photograph by William Swekosky. Missouri Historical Society.*

Right: Nineteenth-century desk displayed at the Pitot House, New Orleans. *Photograph by Rachelle O'Brien.*

it she became. She stopped now and then to dab her swollen eyes and sharpen her pencil with sandpaper.

By 1885, Kate was thirty-five, alone and far away. She would write local color stories about anyone in Louisiana with abandon. Writing was revenge therapy.

Kate missed New Orleans and Grand Isle. But it was Cloutierville, this pleasure-seeking, brazen clump of people, who obsessed her. These rough bayou folk, who thrashed through oven heat and flooding rain, snarled at yellow fever, typhoid, malaria. These nonreaders, who condemned the opera but flung themselves into the wet grass, made love in the fields and raced bareback at dusk.

ASTUTE AUTHOR AND BUSINESSWOMAN

1885–98

Like her artistic contemporary Edgar Degas, ferociously drawing pastels to save his family from bankruptcy, Kate needed to make money for her children.

Kate's compromised real estate in St. Louis couldn't sustain them. She had to earn income in a town she'd left fifteen years before, a town where she'd never made any money—nor been expected to.

Writing, an acceptable profession for women, inspired Kate. But whereas most authors write first and seek publication later, Kate did

Kate Chopin, 1886. *Missouri Historical Society.*

the opposite. She deeply researched what sorts of stories got bought and published. She found that publications, like *Vogue*, the *Atlantic* and *Harper's*, were hunting for larger-than-life folktales. Readers wanted complex stories with exotic places, archetypical characters, big themes and happy endings. That was Louisiana!

Kate wrote within the fairytale umbrella of being a folksy author. She would publish over one hundred short stories, including "A Night in Acadie," "In and Out of Old Natchitoches," "A Lady of Bayou St. John," "Beyond the Bayou," "Ripe Figs," "A No-Account Creole" and "Dr. Chevalier's Lie."[24] Her heart, mind and hand were ignited with the spirit; she wrote nonstop, pouring her love of the bayou into her local color stories, enchanting the world with Louisiana.

Soon, a voice whispered, *Come back to Cloutierville.*

BAYOU COMFORT

Who or what was Kate looking for in Cloutierville? Was it all for research? The town had not changed much since she left in 1884. What was compelling Kate's return: Oscar's relatives, new friends, old ones? Her sisters-in-law, brothers-in-law, the priest and that rancher were all still there.

Kate had corresponded with Cane River relatives, but it was the going back, the presence of the place and people, that revived the feelings. Some

Arbres limitant une plaine (1870–75), Edgar Degas. The exact date of this pastel landscape drawing is unknown. During this time, Degas experienced issues with his eyesight painting outdoors. This landscape resembles Louisiana, and authors propose it could have been created while Degas visited New Orleans. *Donation by Baronne Eva Gebhard-Gourgaud, 1965. © Musée d'Orsay, Dist. RMN-Grand Palais / Patrice Schmidt.*

say that she visited Louisiana fearlessly each year, corresponded with Cane River relatives (like the twenty-three-year-old once-orphaned sister-in-law) and took notes.

Kate visited her in-laws because she had to: Eugenie, Marie and Lamy had gracious mansions. Lamy still managed the impressive, four-thousand-acre family estate. Kate's own house stayed rented. Oscar had failed, his Achilles heel having been mercy, but Lamy had succeeded big, and her sisters-in-law had "married up." Still, Kate went there mostly in hot summers, entertaining her children and finding inspiration for her writing.

Kate was becoming a well-known author, and for one of her visits, her sister-in-law got her tremendous coverage in the local newspapers. Notices said she was a beautiful and talented literary genius who'd lived many years in the parish. Most locals fawned over her (though some still resented her).

MORE BAYOU LOVE, MORE BAYOU PAIN

We wonder if during those small-town visits, she saw the rancher, intentionally or unintentionally? Love lingers longest when you are shattered by the loss. No one knew how much Kate even thought about him. But Lord knows she remembered that he'd once saved her.

A horseman, still fit and muscular, he'd shown little physical decline. His was the kind of body that white silk shirts should drip off of. In this town of dullards, he was a magnet for the excitable. But they had to catch him in mid-air.

In Cloutierville, love was not a thing; love was a *who*. Before, the galloping manhood of him had magnetized her. This horseman had been her center, foundation, beginning and end.

To guard her heart, Kate had to guard the people who had access to it. And if she collided into this cowboy, she couldn't lose her balance. Spin in the air. Self-destruct. She'd been attracted to him as if to a bright lamppost at night because he had loved her back from the pit of destruction. But she could do without him now.

Relentless, the horseman could have easily pursued Kate, called out to her riding in the fields under stormy, puffed, voluptuous skies. But more probably, he bumped into her at her brother-in-law's large, gracious mansion, where Kate mostly stayed. The rancher liked to show off his women, and Lamy liked to show off his cash. Lamy threw house parties for friends and relatives, transporting them by steamer, train or buggy to his manor. In small towns, the super wealthy tended to know each other.

But Kate eventually learned the rancher had moved on for good. He was cohabitating with the blonde vixen, three years younger than Kate, three times as rough. He'd set her up in a lovely house, paid her bills, given her the amethyst-tinted hurricane lamp (that Kate had given him). He even gifted her his most valuable land—saying it was in exchange for her sewing.

We imagine that when Kate realized their status, the confirmation of that lust-turned-partnership cannonballed her. Did Kate hope their spirits would suffer, groan inside their full coupled bodies? Did she cry her eyes out, feel empty and alone, have days where she didn't eat or barely slept? No magic pill could cure heartbreak. The cowboy left a gaping hole in her already bleeding heart. Nightmares poured dirt into it.

Hot summer days in Cloutierville erupted in violent thunderstorm nights. She'd stay indoors and play solitaire relentlessly to fill up her insides. Perhaps when she relaxed at her in-laws' weathered gray mansion with its galleries,

Right: Kate Chopin (1890–1909). *Missouri Historical Society.*

Below: Pitot House, balcony overlooking Bayou St. John. St. Francis Cabrini, the first American saint, purchased this house in 1904. In 1962, her missionary Sisters of the Sacred Heart donated the building to the Louisiana Landmarks Society. *Photograph by Rachelle O'Brien.*

looking out at the peculiarly light blue, almost white, skies, she could feel the warm breath of the brown river beyond.

Kate was determined to capture something each time she came back. Once, in her upset, she decided to take Oscar's body away from Cloutierville back to St. Louis. She buried him in Calvary Cemetery on April 26, 1889, in the O'Flaherty plot. Maybe she wanted Oscar nearby for the children. Perhaps it was an act of revenge. But having Oscar's coffin in St. Louis (in an unmarked grave) didn't stop Kate from returning to Cloutierville.

THE AWAKENING IN LOUISIANA

Later, in June 1897, Kate visited Louisiana for a long time during the same month she began writing her explosive novel, *The Awakening*: a story about a woman with active sexual desires who seeks independence and self-fulfillment, a woman who dares to leave her husband and have an affair.

It was hot hot that summer when Kate arrived with her seventeen-year-old daughter. Almost child-free (her boys were now twenty to twenty-seven), Kate had been widowed for fifteen years and possessed freedom, psychologically and physiologically. Were her fantasies luring her into dreaming again?

What was forty-seven-year-old Kate looking for in the folds of steamy grass, loose magnolias dropping from trees, wide moss-burdened oak trees? Why had she needed to breathe in the humid air, look up at the dark night sky, ride the fields on a wild mare?

Did she want to catch a glimpse of the handsome rancher? Rumor was, even at fifty-three, he was still roaming the Louisiana fields, drinking, driving his stallion, drifting on a whim to Colorado and New Orleans. Did she dare touch his body, let her fingers caress his frame, which had not been darkened by the effects of wild living? His stamina, like Kate's imagination, was still unmatchable.

Memories began compelling Kate to write about the magnetism of love, writing in 1898:

> *One really never knows the exact, definite thing which excites love for any person, and one can never truly know whether this love is the result of circumstances, or whether it is predestination.*

Half-Naked Woman, Seen from Behind, Combing her Hair, a Mirror Reflecting Her Body, Berthe Morisot, unknown date. © *RMN-Grand Palais (Musée d'Orsay)*.

I am inclined to think that loves springs from animal instinct, and therefore, is, in a measure, divine. One can never resolve to love this man, this woman or child, and then carry out the resolution, unless one feels irresistibly drawn by an indefinable current of magnetism....

But I am sure we all feel that love—true, pure, love, is an uncontrollable emotion that allows of no analyzation and no vivisection.[25]

Kate planned to spend the entire summer at her sister-in-law's large and decorous home, but she aborted the trip and returned quickly to Missouri. No one knows why.

But shortly afterward, Kate secretly penciled in her journal a sexual story about the ripe desire between ex-lovers in a thunderstorm. Here, an unstoppable union explodes between the French Creole rancher and the Acadian woman. Perhaps Kate recalled the strong, long-armed horseman, roughly dressed, muscles bulging.

Did Kate realize how embedded he was in her flesh? Both of them had a need for intimate conjugal life, a stormy cyclone that raged without and within them—just like the couple inside the rain. Kate's closest allies were her adult children and her relatives, but could she tell them her fantasies? No, it was too dangerous to reveal this part of herself. She refused to publish this story in her lifetime. "The Storm" was her secret to keep.

Last Visits

The following chilly Christmas season of 1898, Kate was lured back to Louisiana. A year had passed, in which she'd finished writing the most revealing work of her life, which no one there had yet read. Her friends didn't know her novel's sexual, dark, feminist underbelly. *The Awakening* would soon be published, in 1899.

Daily, even hourly, Louisiana had preyed on Kate's mind. She wasn't ready to stop loving the state.

We suspect Kate went back to Cloutierville to inhale it one more time while she still felt comfortable traveling, while her eyes and ears could still revel in the night-blooming gardenias. She didn't want to admit her health was compromised. Only here would she soak up the glory of the magnolias with their voluptuous scent, the camelias that burst open, the pansies, honeysuckle, violas that lifted their heads to the gentle rain.

Once, Kate had enjoyed Cloutierville's Round Table Club meetings, whist and euchre parties, with special cakes and baby dolls as prizes. She was always laughing, smoking into the wee hours with her in-laws on the bayou. Kate was misanthropic, both loving and hating socializing, both loving cards and despising frivolous chatter. But now, she tired more easily. No matter; she remained daring, socializing, sitting with skirt riding up, legs crossed, flaunting her cigarette and her hair cut short.

She was there to end a part of her life, so she could sail into the future. To sell the farmhouse where her daughter had been born, so she could finance her debut. But relatives were flabbergasted. Lamy (who wanted to buy up all Kate's land for his Louisiana empire) had wanted the house, but Kate sold it instead to a German merchant, who offered her a better price. Selling her home in Cloutierville severed Kate's link to Louisiana.

Kate had planned a longer visit, but within a week, she aborted her stay and departed. She fled, disrupting the visit, lest like Lot's wife in the Bible she look back and be turned into salt.

Chapter 10

STRONG WINGS

The bird that would soar above the level plane
of tradition and prejudice must have strong wings.[26]
—*Kate Chopin*

AMONG THE LITERARY ELITE

Yes, Kate had to get back to civility once again, smother her mourning for Louisiana inside gracious St. Louis society and her weekly salon. Writing became Kate's holy comforter and the growing writing community her sacred elixir. She became a literary icon in St. Louis, although she set her popular short stories defiantly and exclusively in Louisiana.

Kate had been willing to walk away from Louisiana and keep on walking. She had seen sudden and slow deaths. She didn't have time to punish anybody. There was likely a period when she would rather have died than not visit Louisiana.

She had had to take notes, gain clarity, squeeze the feelings that surged into words. Kate had always kept a toe in the pond of Louisiana. She set her stories exclusively there, infused her male characters with the horseman, as if he were an obsession, audaciously using his name in full or abbreviated form throughout her many tales.

Back in her St. Louis chrysalis, Kate was free to write, to dare, to dream. She could create whichever characters and worlds she pleased. Writing was her defense against heartbreak.

Kate Chopin (1890–99).
Photograph by H. Holborn.
Missouri Historical Society.

The test had been to live inside her complex characters' feelings and speak truer truths about what she saw. Be the puppet and the puppeteer at the most intimate moments. Kate wrote,

Perhaps, it is better to wake up after all, even to suffer, rather than to remain a dupe to illusions of one's life.[27]

Would she write in dangerous, truthful, feminist territory?

SLAUGHTERED REPUTATION

Kate finished her novel *The Awakening* (first entitled *A Solitary Soul*) in January 1898. She proclaimed the story of a New Orleans woman, seeking to shamelessly commit to her creative, spiritual and sexual needs. She endangers herself by abandoning her Creole cotton broker husband and children for a passionate affair.

Writing this novel, did Kate realize how embedded the horseman was in her flesh? They both had a need for privacy: hers with books, his with land. But critics didn't care for her Alcée Arobin character, or Edna Pontellier.

In April 1899, shocked reviews filled the papers, calling Kate's novel sordid, morbid, unhealthy and poisonous. Critics defamed *The Awakening* for its immoral female protagonist, who went unpunished for her sins. Ugly notices kept slamming the novel as a sex book. Friends cringed, wishing they could comfort Kate. Her four children living at home tried, as did her literary salon. Soon, Kate's publisher joined the hate team and canceled the contract for her next collection of stories, *A Vocation and a Voice*. It had been too dangerous for Kate to write so exposed in her forties, without youth, beauty, man-power buttressing her.

We imagine Kate's belief in herself plunged. Did she stop reading reviews, for the agony they inflicted? Writers can't really reverse the attack, repudiate criticism. Kate's reputation was slaughtered overnight.

Bravely Forward

Scorned as a sex writer, Kate had to face the debutante season and support her daughter in finding a husband, just as Kate's mother had for her.

Kate likely hated presenting Lélia the year of Kate's shaming. Part of Kate's complexity was: she complied. Hoping someone would still want to marry her daughter, Kate accompanied her to debutante social gatherings, smiling at ladies in delicate, lacy tea dresses and men peacocked into fishtail tuxedoes, their high, round-collared shirts stiff to the chest. People probably smirked, looked down and walked away.

Failing Health and the Losing Game

Kate began having migraines, heart palpitations, breathlessness. She developed a cough from three decades as a smoker. And no, she wouldn't quit smoking her Cuban cigarettes. Some said she was experiencing vision issues and shortness of breath. Maybe she blamed the dirty, unpredictable weather conditions.

Depressed, she clung to her children and dreaded leaving home. With no escape to Louisiana possible, Kate, like the poet Baudelaire, went mostly silent.

Did anyone notice that Kate began to get her affairs in order? She wrote a will in December 1902, being sure to leave her house to her daughter. (She was likely relieved when Lélia received a marriage proposal.)

Kate's sons started leaving home; her eldest, Jean, moved out with his jubilant, pregnant wife.

But death was stalking Kate. Her daughter-in-law and new grandbaby died in childbirth, and Jean sunk into deep depression, from which he never recovered. He crawled home and moved back in to the comforting womb of mama.

KATE'S COLLAPSE

Then, on one of the hottest days in St. Louis, Kate trekked to the 1904 World's Fair's Louisiana Purchase Exposition. Her five sons, all grown and still living in St. Louis, had probably encouraged her to rest, not go out.

Kate probably never thought when she walked out of her house on Morgan Street that it'd be for the last time. If she was strong enough to go to the fair, she was strong enough to come back upright. Wasn't she? But the highly trafficked fair was packed with 200,000 people in 1,200 acres of thickets. And Kate collapsed.

Her symptoms swiftly worsened. That night at home, she cried out for her children. A cerebral hemorrhage had felled her. Did she suspect when she went unconscious on Sunday, August 21, 1904, that she'd never stand up or write again, never whisper goodbye to the people in St. Louis and Louisiana she so loved?

In her middle years (fifty-four), like her mother (dead at fifty-six), Kate was gone. Heartache had taken a toll on her physical health, literally causing her heart to break. Her soul soared in God-flight to the heavens.

Summer heat increased putrefaction, so Kate was buried quickly, before the horror of her loss struck her children in the gut, before they read her obituary: "Mrs. Kate Chopin Died Suddenly Today." Loved ones celebrated her at a Catholic requiem Mass and buried her at the Calvary Cemetery beside her daughter-in-law and newborn, with places saved for her children, to be buried around her.

Kate's children likely faced a profusion of unwanted callers, bill collectors, busybodies, whom Kate would have dismissed with a stern smile. Her bereft children had to learn to live with that uncomfortable, confused, painful and somewhat guilty feeling that creeps back sometimes. No hope. No healing. No mental morphine possible. When Kate died, her children shrunk inside their grief. They weren't just mourning Kate's death; they were dealing with the trauma of her absence, the loss of her giantness, her humor, curiosity, determination, discipline, wisdom, intelligence, kindness, courage, the encyclopedia of talents that she was.

LOUISIANA IMPACT

What was Kate's impact after her spirit left this earth? Did her children lose their southern connection? Kate had guarded their childhoods in

Louisiana. None of them ever moved back to Cloutierville. Kate had kept Louisiana alive through action, writing the stories, visiting the places, iconifying the people. But Louisiana seemed to lose its influence on her children. Gone were the Louisiana lullabies Kate sang to them, gone were the ferocious thunderstorms pounding the roof, gone were the Creole aunts, uncles and cousins who cherished them. Louisiana was gone with the death of their mother.

Louisiana relatives couldn't make the funeral (if they were even invited). No time to send out white vellum grief cards, bordered in black. No time to send Kate's photograph, locket of hair or a shadow box with mementos (if anyone even asked for them). Did her in-laws travel to St. Louis to comfort Kate's children or visit her tiny, barely marked grave? Probably not. Kate had been the glue, the inconvenienced one, traveling with her brood of children year after year.

In Cloutierville, the passing of Kate Chopin had been small. No town crier marched down the road screaming out her death. No rituals solidified it. No stopped clock, no covered mirror, no window opened to let the spirit fly out, no death wreath hung on the door, no church bell tolled. No washing and laying out of the body, no sitting up for days by the casket, no digging of a grave, no solemn mass, no procession to the cemetery, no empty family home to make you cross yourself when you passed.

Back on Main Street, some were relieved. Kate had made men feel breathless and women worthless, with her cigarettes, her horses, her tiger-raging nerves. Some foes gloated that her works would be forgotten, as indeed they were for fifty years. Those withering inside their small lives smirked endlessly.

Everybody went back to their normal lives, but for some, like the rancher, life would never be as normal-exciting again. Sudden deaths do that, knock people off their pedestals. The horseman didn't have to deal with the horror of post-death duties, close the curtains or cover the mirrors. He didn't have to project his grief through black leather gloves, armband, hat band, dark suit and tie. Unchallenged, he could continue roaming, sink into dreary grandpa-hood, finance his live-in, die in the bed of his first wife.

Up in St. Louis, nothing changed much because Kate had died. The heat continued without her marching through it. The world's fair stayed open without her dreaming inside it. Lélia's wedding inched ahead (small, solemn, but forward) without Kate's participation.

Kate's death had a ripple effect, erasing her and silencing her stories for decades.

Now a ghost, Kate couldn't resurrect her image by wearing extravagant clothes, smoking forbidden cigars, mounting bareback stallions. In death, Kate was finally alone with God and the angels in the sun, listening to the ocean's roar, her face turned upward to gather in the vast expanse of light, her arms raised, meeting and melting in the dazzling sky. Kate was too big for Louisiana. Even the Louisiana of her imagination. Mesmerized but weary, the state stepped to the side.

KATE'S LEGACY

Kate's writing output had been unmatchable. So what if critics slaughtered her, erased her, broke her heart? It was silly to believe they could ever cage her. Strip her books from the shelves. Freeze her mouth. Stop her heart. They were bloody servants to her destiny.

Because on an old bookshelf in Connecticut, a book was opened, its crusty pages read. Indeed, great art nestles in the dust before it is resurrected. Kate's words rebounded in one person's soul, and *The Awakening* was resuscitated. Great artists only need one: one poem, one song, one book and one reader. The rest is in the hands of God.

Fifty years after her death, Kate Chopin peeked out and blossomed worldwide. Let her ride.

PART II

◇ ◇ ◇

MORE SECRETS ABOUT KATE CHOPIN

Chapter 1

WE JUST CAN'T LET YOU GO, KATE!

Our book is not a biography of Kate Chopin. Plenty of brilliant scholars and historians have written those. Rather, we your authors, daughters of New Orleans, show how Kate's experience in our home state deeply affected her identity and her writing.

Included in the back matter of this book are interviews with scholars, experts and descendants, who informed our research. But before we get into more of the research, first let's connect with the soul of an artist.

Chapter 2

THE SOUL OF AN ARTIST

Poetry by Barret O'Brien

The enchanting poetry of Barret O'Brien is included because like Mark Duplass (our foreword author), Barret is a huge talent and native New Orleanian. Okay, okay, we are also Barret's mother and sister (nepotism proclaimed), so we know how hard Barret works and the sacrifices he has made for his art. Barret has lived, loved and forged through New Orleans and many other places across the world, including New York City, London, Los Angeles, New Haven, Ashland and Missoula. He is prolific: a poet, novelist, screenwriter, filmmaker, director and a Yale School of Drama–trained actor.

Barret's masterful writing shows us that, like Kate, he knows what it means to be inside and outside a relationship, a partner and an ex-partner, a parent and a loner, a beloved friend and an exile. His wry humor exposes an understanding of life that is magical, heart-wrenching and, indeed, profound. We dance and sing when we hear his words—as surely we would have had we had the opportunity to hear Kate proclaim hers out loud.

We are deeply honored to share Barret's ripe poetry with you, as the themes of these poems resonate with Kate Chopin. His words shimmer inside the world of now New Orleans, as well as the universe that Kate once inhabited. We know that, like Kate, Barret will one day have his voice amplified all over the world. We salute him and all artists, dreamers and writers from Louisiana. And we include him in celebration of those who carry the Chopin torch.

THE COLUMNS HOTEL

A soft story.
   One with a happy ending.
   Where one girl holds one boy's affection,
   and the coffee stays hot in the cup.
    "Let's distribute the populace,"
   the boy says to the girl,
    "So that no guitarist ever plays to an empty room."
   The girl just smiles,
    "He's a dreamer," she thinks.
   They touch feet under the table.
   A bird lands on a branch then flies away again.
   A breeze blows
   and they're content.
   To sit
   and breathe.

MY GREEN DESK

why write?
every day?
the world, with its bulging waistline
needs not another sonnet.
then again, it needed not the first
nor the second
yet they wrote.
their world as perfect as mine
yet they rose
to write
a few choice words
to understand
and try to make more beautiful
in our understanding.
the peacock wants to be gawked at
wants to hear our audible gasp
as we grasp for description.
so i will try.
i will bring this desk to try.

SOME

Of those
who've been
tossed aside,
held back,
skimmed over,
rolled by,
kicked out,
knocked down,
seen through,
licked,
sunk,
hung to dry,
left
   to rot,
some
   get up.
Again.
  Re newed.
  Re vigored.
Simpler.
Better.
Stronger.
More empathetic.
  Now,
of their time,
  their city,
  their vocation.
They met pain,
  self-doubt,
  self-obsession,
  self-regret.
Saw through it.
  Over.
  Past.
Rose above it.

Chapter 3

EXPERTS REFLECT ON
THE CHOPIN MYSTERIES

Interview with Dr. Thomas Bonner, Chopin Scholar

Dr. Thomas Bonner is a professor emeritus in the Department of English at Xavier University in New Orleans, Louisiana. A scholar on Kate Chopin, he wrote *The Kate Chopin Companion: With Chopin's Translations from French Fiction* (1988), based on decades of his research. This resource includes a dictionary of characters, places and terms from Kate's life and writings, as well as period maps of Louisiana and Missouri. Dr. Bonner is also an esteemed contributor to the Kate Chopin International Society.

How did you come to start studying Kate Chopin's work?

I was drawn to her when I was about fourteen, when I read "Desirée's Baby" on a streetcar going home from Jesuit high school. As a typical fourteen-year-old, the exotic interested me. It was 1956, before public accommodations came in 1964, and I was sitting on a segregated streetcar. It struck me that her story is very much about color in the sense of identifying race. And here I was, sitting in front of a "For Colored Only" sign. It struck me that there were people sitting in front of the sign who were darker than people who were sitting in back of the sign.

In 1969, I was taking a seminar (at Tulane University) with Dr. Donald Pizer on American literature of the 1890s. On the first day, Dr. Pizer sent a list of writers around the table that we might consider working on. I saw Kate Chopin, but there was somebody else's name next to it. So I talked to the young woman who had put her name there, and I wound up trading with her, providing that I would tutor her in Old English for six weeks. So I wrote a seminar paper, which was basically an exploratory paper on Chopin. I went on to do my dissertation, continuing to work on Kate Chopin in 1975.

What was the focus of your dissertation?

It was essentially on the formal compositional element of Chopin's two novels and her short stories. I looked at the characterization, structure, point of view, narrative technique and themes of those works.

What has surprised you when studying the works of Kate Chopin?

When I was fourteen, I was shocked by the idea of miscegenation. I still think "Desirée's Baby" is a powerful story. It's not set in New Orleans but near Natchitoches, Louisiana. A female sensibility is what I discovered in reading her.

When you're reading *The Awakening* and you are dealing with Edna and Adèle, you're looking at their having some common views but some significantly different views about their lives. Edna is talking about herself as a person, beyond being a wife, beyond being a mother. Adèle is talking about herself intertwined largely with the life of her husband and her children.

If there was one thing that somewhat stays with me beyond some of the racial elements, it's that. I'm from a family of boys—I have three brothers, and we grew up on a military base. I can honestly say that it took a great deal of time before I began to realize that my mother really had a very different self that wasn't evident on a daily basis. She had gone to Newcomb College and majored in Latin. And she was a great reader. She had an intellectual life apart from her daily life as an officer's wife in the army and that of a mother.

Can you tell us more about teaching Kate Chopin at Xavier University?

I've taught *The Awakening* in seminars and American literature survey courses and have taught Chopin in the context of Southern literature, women writers and largely American writers. It always has had good and often intriguing responses from the students. Xavier is an interesting school because it's very New Orleans.

What are some of your approaches to teaching Kate Chopin?

When I taught Chopin in the context of American literature, we talked about realism. Writers used dialect, and some exploited dialect. But I don't think Chopin was one of those for sure. She simply was using her ear to the best of her ability. There is this directness in portraying human experience.

At the same time, I don't find that Chopin used dialect in an intensive way. I always thought it was rather lightly used, compared to many others—even Mark Twain. It was in vogue then to try to capture the exact way to use words—as opposed to now, when dialogue is pretty much all the same.

Can you tell us more about some of the places in New Orleans that existed when Kate Chopin lived there?

The opera house was really big in New Orleans. It was big in New Orleans before it was big in New York. Kate did go to the opera here. She was musically inclined. I mean, she actually did write a piece of music, called *Lilia*, after one of her children. The Opera House burned down in about 1917 or 1918. So it doesn't exist anymore.

Chopin lived basically in the American parts of the city. Her last house was a duplex on Louisiana Avenue, and she lived in several other houses before. There was a little one just below the Garden District. You know, she obviously walked a bit in the city. Emily Toth has written about that.

Chopin had a real sense of the city: for example, the house she uses for *The Awakening* was on Esplanade Avenue. Do you have Bernie Koloski's edition of *The Awakening*? Because there's a picture of a house that she no doubt used for *The Awakening*.

Double cottage that scholars Bonner and Koloski referenced. In *The Awakening*, Chopin writes, "The Pontelliers possessed a very charming home on Esplanade Street in New Orleans. It was a large, double cottage, with a broad front veranda, whose round, fluted columns supported the sloping roof." *Photograph provided by permission of Ashton's Bed and Breakfast, New Orleans.*

Since she began writing as a child, do you think she probably wrote while she lived in Louisiana?

She may have written a little bit. She may have done letters and so forth, but she was busy. I think she was married in 1869, and she arrived here in '70 and then was here until '79. And she was having children and was also socially active. In terms of her husband, he was a cotton factor, which involved probably frequent social gatherings and so forth, then going to the opera.

My wife and I had two children. She is a painter and an art historian, and during that period of rearing children, there were periods when she could hardly get any of that kind of work done. Kate must have had similar interruptions to her writing life.

Kate got up to Cloutierville in '79; she stayed there until '84. Then she went to St. Louis, where she began to generate herself as a writer. Her period of writing really was not down here, but up in St. Louis.

How was Kate Chopin received fifty years ago? Why do you think she is still relevant today?

In 1969, Chopin was being revived on the basis of the women's movement. I thought that was important, but I also thought that there was research that went beyond a thematic approach to her work. And so that's how I did the compositional work for the dissertation, and it led to examining other areas of her work.

That emphasis on the women's movement is really important. For example, *Red Book* magazine in the early seventies published *The Awakening* in its entirety in a single issue.

At this point, we are dealing with Chopin, whose work is seen as a fixture in American literature. She is not new. She doesn't have the revolutionary ardor about her work among readers and scholars. So there's an edge that's been sort of pulled off. She's there, along with Melville and everybody else. And what's interesting about her is that Chopin wrote two novels and something over one hundred short stories and she's considered a major writer. In the mid-twentieth century, major writers had to have written multiple novels, like James, Wharton, Hawthorne and Faulkner. Whereas we have a major writer, Chopin, with two novels and just over one hundred short stories. So there's been a revision in terms of how we look at what's major and what's minor.

Is there anything that you wish people would research about Kate Chopin's work or her life, or any question you feel hasn't yet been answered about Kate Chopin?

There's a Mexican impulse in *The Awakening*, with Robert going there. One of the things that interests me is Americans [traveling to Mexico] in terms of their business experiment. So often, a lot of the French names started to get Anglicized. When Robert goes down to Mexico for business, he's withdrawing from his association with Edna because things were getting very difficult socially. The Mexican connection has not been fully developed in studies of her work.

There was a considerable relationship between New Orleans and Mexico across the nineteenth century. At one time, there was even an attempt to make a land trail for trade between Mexico and New Orleans.

INTERVIEW WITH DR. C.W. CANNON, NEW ORLEANS STUDIES SCHOLAR

Dr. C.W. Cannon teaches courses in New Orleans studies at Loyola University New Orleans. His latest book is *I Want Magic: Essays on New Orleans, the South, and Race* (2022). A Fulbright scholar, his pantheon of work includes New Orleans novels (*Soul Resin, Katrina Means Cleansing, French Quarter Beautification Project* and *Sleepytime Down South*), as well as anthologies (*Louisiana in Words* and *Do You Know What It Means to Miss New Orleans*). He is a frequent contributor to the *Lens* (thelensnola.org).

What is your view of The Awakening *as a novel?*

My view of *The Awakening* is that it's a novel of the artist, what the Germans call a *Künstlerroman*. It's a specific type of bildungsroman, or coming-of-age novel, more frequent on the European continent than it is in the United States. It's specifically about becoming an artist and about the struggle to become an artist.

What inspires you about Chopin's The Awakening?

From my personal connection, it's the way that it shows Edna's aesthetic experience, the aesthetic dimension of her personality. I see Edna as an artist. In the novel, an artist is defined by temperament. You're born that way. You can't become an artist by trying. That is the Romantic conception of the artist. It's not about whether you're producing or selling art; it's whether you have an aesthetic temperament. I kind of agree with that, too. And that's what the novel's all about. That's why I like it the most. This novel is one of the great novels about the life of an artist in all American literature.

What's unique about the world that Kate Chopin creates in The Awakening?

It's a mythic space that Chopin creates for Edna Pontellier. It's an elite White Creole bubble, it's a very fanciful space that serves the purpose of her narrative. It's definitely Creole culture. There are certain things about the society we see among elite New Orleanians at the time the novel is set, like vacationing in Grand Isle, that she's specific about.

One of the interesting things about *The Awakening* is how devoid it is of political and social details of the time. It's kind of odd, as all the other writers of her generation who write about New Orleans, they paid a lot more attention to the social and political scene, like George Washington Cable, Alice Dunbar Nelson and Grace King. But Chopin includes nothing about any of the political situation at all, which is a little strange. Then again, Kate had been gone (from Louisiana) for about twenty years when she wrote the novel, so she might not have even really been keeping up with the politics.

Can you tell us more about Kate Chopin's influences?

The Awakening is a Symbolist novel. There are other novels that preceded *The Awakening* that deal with similar subject matter, like *Anna Karenina*. Anna Karenina kills herself. There's a German version by Theodor Fontane, where the woman also kills herself. And there are others. The original may have been Gustave Flaubert's *Madame Bovary*. Women characters who kill themselves for love go back as far as Virgil's *Aeneid*, where Dido kills herself upon Aeneas's departure from Carthage, but the nineteenth-century storylines are concerned with a social critique of patriarchal society; that's probably the difference.

Women rebels of desire exist in this common narrative and always kill themselves. During the time these novels were published, Emma Goldman was a radical anarchist feminist and was traveling all across the country. She even visited New Orleans and delivered a lecture called "Marriage and Love," in which she excoriates marriage. She says that marriage and love are incompatible. Marriage is a sucker's game. It enslaves women.

This was a very common line of thinking at that time on the part of feminist radicals of the era of the late nineteenth century. This is not something new that Chopin's character Edna thinks up that no one else has gone through in the 1890s.

Can you tell us more about Creole culture?

Some interpreters of *The Awakening* see it as a critique of a certain kind of conservative old Creole society, but it's basically the patriarchal culture of the old bourgeoisie throughout the Western world, not specific to New Orleans. And if anything, the Creoles are less patriarchal than the Americans are.

From Edna's perspective, Creoles' freedom of expression was at first incomprehensible to her. Creoles talk about private, personal, physical matters—and sex—with each other very openly. Edna is not used to that. Maybe that plays a role in her awakening.

Another aspect to note is her sensual attraction to Adèle Ratignolle, the beautiful Creole Madonna of the novel. It's very erotic, the way Edna sees Adèle, the language she uses and the way she sees her. Her feelings for her are described in interesting ways that sound a lot like romantic love. My whole interpretation of the novel is not limited to her sexual liberation, though. I see the sexual liberation as symptomatic of her broader quest to become an artist, to experience the world as an artist does.

So Edna's first drawn to Adèle because as an artist, she has artistic inclination. She has the temperament already. And she's already got an artist's eye. So this is the cause of her sensuous susceptibility to beauty; the excessive physical charm of Adèle attracted her. So excessive physical charm just means she's gorgeous! Edna is noticing the openness that these Creoles have that she's not used to. She's realizing that she has repressed things her whole life.

I do think that being in the Creole milieu is what puts the central character, Edna Pontellier, in the mindset to have her awakening. In other words, I think it's doubtful that if Edna had stayed in Kentucky, where her father currently lived, or Mississippi, where she had grown up, she ever would have had her awakening. The Creole embrace of sensuality and the aesthetic dimension of daily life is what triggers her.

When does Edna's awakening begin?

The immediate trigger of her awakening is a huge clue, occurring during a prelude by Frederic Chopin, performed by Mademoiselle Reisz. That's when her awakening kicks into high gear.

The awakening takes part over the course of one night. It's August 28; Chopin even gives it a date. After that, she's changed, and it takes her a little while to catch up and figure out how she's changed. But she knows that something happened on that night.

At one point, she says her anchorage had been loosening, and on that night, the chains snapped, which allowed her to drift wherever her newly awakened unconscious took her. It's the night of Mademoiselle Reisz's performance of Chopin. We know it's a Chopin prelude, because audience members say so after the recital (I surmise that it's the *Prelude No. 24 in D Minor.*) Chopin wrote:

> *But the very passions themselves were aroused within her soul, swaying it, lashing it, as the waves daily beat upon her splendid body.*

Was there something about New Orleans that sparks the artistic awakening in her character in Edna?

Chopin's writing is particularly loaded with the tragic apprehension of the *sublime* because Edna's trying to become an artist. We might say: "What kind of artist?" The conception of the artist in this novel is decidedly the Romantic artist.

I think that the novel's understanding of what art is is rooted in Romantic aesthetics, dating back to Edmund Burke and Immanuel Kant's discussion of how a great work of art should contain elements of the beautiful and the sublime.

Great art should have both: it should be beautiful, which is to say pretty, magnetic or captivating. It holds our interest. We're drawn to it. That's the beautiful part. But a finally crafted article of furniture is also beautiful. A chocolate cake is beautiful. And fashion is, presumably, beautiful. So the distinction is that none of those crafts has the sublime dimension.

The sublime is the scary part of art. The sublime is that element of art that reminds us of the tragedy of the human condition: that we are basically meaningless specks of dust in the scope of the universe and a hundred years from now, nobody will care about our lives. This is upsetting knowledge, that our lives are ultimately meaningless. The Romantic artist must grapple with this and must find a way to somehow package that in a digestible form for audiences.

Is The Awakening *primarily about gender, or does it go beyond?*

In chapter 6, Chopin presents the categories of Edna's position in the universe as a human being and her social situation: being a woman in society. She also refers to Edna's relation to the world within: that's her unconscious.

And this is where I think it goes beyond gender. You know, there's a tendency to ghettoize great women's fiction and just make it just about women's issues. The character is a woman. Women's issues are obviously part of the world she's navigating. But it does it a disservice to suggest that what Edna's experiencing is not something that is experienced by all human beings who struggle to become artists. Her gender places limits on her that men would not experience, though men might experience other limitations. But her "position in the universe as a human being" is a broader category than her position in society as a woman.

Edna's recognition of her position in the universe as a human being is the upsetting, disturbing apprehension of the sublime. She is realizing the fact that our lives are starkly limited, even beyond social limitations, and we don't really have control over what happens to us.

How did Kate Chopin write about race?

Some native writers of Louisiana at the time obsessively explored the meaning of race. But this wasn't the case for Kate Chopin. It's odd how absent any kind of racial analysis is from the novel.

There's a great line in *The Awakening* that I share in my classes. We also do a similar exercise in my classes when we study Tennessee Williams, because he doesn't write much directly about race either, but you can detect clues of the White racial unconscious in both authors.

In the first chapter, Mr. Pontellier sees their children being followed around by a quadroon nurse described as having a "far away" air. What does this descriptor tell us about the narrative point of view? The Black nanny is not "far away" as much as the narrative point of view feels "far away" from any and all Black characters. It tells us that Black New Orleanians were likely a cipher to Chopin; she has no idea. She doesn't have any kind of longing to understand, either. She just doesn't have any feelings about it but occasionally adopts some embarrassing stereotypes (as in chapter 20) since her imagination of Blackness is so empty, probably from a lack of personal experience.

The Awakening*'s ending is tragic, with the protagonist's death. But do you think is it possible that Edna doesn't commit suicide?*

Everybody seems to think that Edna kills herself. It's the common reading. This is the way I look at the ending, too: I think it probably is a suicide. But if we think that the reason that she kills herself is because of an inability to have an independent sexual life, I think that that doesn't add up. That makes the ending stupid. It makes Edna pathetic, and it seems she would be really lacking in courage and imagination.

However, there's another way of looking at it. And that way is that it's a symbolic apotheosis in the end, just like at the end of *Tristan and Isolde*, another big opera of the era of illicit love. In the end, Isolde inexplicably collapses.

Edna has been toying around with this idea of the sublime and also the longing she has, apparently, for oblivion. It's too much of a struggle to be in constant touch with the longing of her unconscious. Her repressive apparatus is shattered. Today, we would easily diagnose her with clinical depression. But in the service of the novel, it's more philosophical.

It's the idea that she wants to have this union with the universe. You know, she wants to embrace the universe and all and the depths of her unconscious, which has been symbolized by the sea from the beginning. The sea is obviously her unconscious. The unconscious is as vast as the universe, as depthless as the universe. So when Edna wades into the ocean in the end, this is a symbolic apotheosis of her embracing a loss of self in order to become free.

INTERVIEW WITH DR. BARBARA EWELL, CHOPIN SCHOLAR

Dr. Barbara Ewell is a leading scholar on Kate Chopin (1850–1904). Her books and editions include *Kate Chopin*; *The Awakening and Other Writings by Kate Chopin*; *Sweet Spots: In Between Spaces in New Orleans*; *Southern Local Color: Stories of Region, Race and Gender*; *Voices of the American South*; and *The Anthology of Spanish American Thought and Culture*. Dr. Ewell is a professor emerita of at Loyola University New Orleans.

What do you think really made you fall in love with Kate Chopin as a writer?

The Awakening. Reading that novel was like a revelation. I did love her writing. When I started reading some of her short stories, I was even more delighted, mainly because of the Cajun material. My family is Cajun—despite my Welsh surname—and I dedicated my book on Chopin to my parents,

"Children of bayou folk." The people Kate Chopin was writing about were, in some sense, my people. So it was very personal in many ways; besides, Chopin was a woman writer who had been lost, and all of the excitement about that recovery was going on in the 1970s and 1980s. I was just thrilled to be part of that discovery.

How would you describe Cajun people from that part of Louisiana?

First, a bit of history. In the middle of the eighteenth century, the Cajun people were dislocated by the English from Nova Scotia: Le Grand Dérangement. When they were thrown out of Acadia, many ended up in French Louisiana, where as farmers and peasants, they were given an ambivalent welcome.

Gradually, most of them moved into the south Louisiana hinterlands up and down its many bayous, to farm and raise cattle. Because it's Louisiana, of course—incredibly fertile and rich with natural resources—they did fine. They were pretty isolated, however, and they largely maintained their traditional culture, adapted to the very different climate as well as to the local Indigenous people and African Americans.

But they were basically off to themselves. They didn't have to make a lot of money because Louisiana offered such an easy living. I mean, the resources were all around them: fish, a long growing season, fertile land, timber. So there was no real need to get caught up in the American scramble. And of course, they didn't have to learn English. They spoke their own, increasingly distinctive, French. Even my grandmother, who was born in 1882, did not speak English till she was six years old.

I'm working my way toward what seems to me the essence of Cajun culture, which is that wonderful sense that life is good—a very French attitude. As in France even today, eating and drinking and relaxing and retiring early are much more important than making a ton of money. And that spirit transferred here.

Of course, I don't want to idealize Cajun life, because many people were poor and didn't have a lot of education or opportunities, but at the same time, it was a forgiving culture and a comfortable place.

By the beginning of the twentieth century, the oil and timber industries, roads and radios, more or less forced Cajuns to become Americanized. When my mother came along, for example (she was born in 1921), she was forbidden to speak French in school and punished for doing so. So my mother understood a little French, but she never really spoke the language—not least because French was very much also considered "backward"—not at all "modern."

Still, I think Cajun culture has managed to maintain its unique spirit. Few people, even in the depths of Cajun country, speak French anymore, and there is a certain self-consciousness about the culture. But the revival of Cajun folklore, its music and food, keeps it alive. In the early seventies, when folks realized we were about to lose something precious, Les Blank made a movie about Cajuns, called *Spend It All*. I mean, what are you saving it for? That, I think, is a key to the Cajun spirit: Spend it all.

As you taught Kate Chopin in New Orleans, and you're a woman from Louisiana, how did you go about it a little bit differently as a local?

I was attracted to her as a feminist, certainly, or a proto-feminist, as we like to say. But I was also, as I think most people are, delighted to see familiar places—ourselves—reflected in fiction, in books.

My roots in Louisiana and New Orleans—I did bring that to my teaching. I know I did, not just here, but when I was teaching in Mississippi and elsewhere; I allowed myself to assume a kind of authority: "I'm sorry, people. My father speaks with an accent like that. My relatives have names like Rema and Odile and Bertrand. I do know something about this." And so, for better or worse, I think, I positioned myself as someone who knows. Of course, I really didn't—and don't—want to claim too much. I certainly didn't grow up speaking Cajun French, though I did eat a lot of crawfish and boudin. But there is a way in which I think I do understand the landscape and the customs and the spirit of Kate's subject matter, maybe with just a little bit of internal familiarity.

How did your students respond to Kate Chopin's works?

In my thirty-plus years at Loyola, I certainly taught a lot of Louisianians, and they were often surprised. I mean, they were often like: *Wow, really? Look at these characters who come out of my experience or share something of my history.* It's like encountering in fiction something familiar: you are drawn to it because it's telling you something about yourself or your history. We do love hearing about ourselves. In that way, many of them responded differently to the general ambiance and the environment of the story. They were amused and delighted—especially by the idea that Grand Isle was a resort, since the place today is hardly that! But as for the issues that Chopin raised, many of those students were as conflicted as readers everywhere: *Should Edna really have killed herself? Wasn't she a bad mother?* And, of course, in the short stories, as well.

How do you feel that Kate Chopin was received in Cloutierville, given her background being from New Orleans and St. Louis?

Emily Toth talks about this point at great length, that Kate wasn't terribly well received. She came with her husband, who was a native, but they were still basically outsiders. Oscar's mother was from a local family, and he was born there, but his father was an émigré from France. It's like: You can't turn them away, they're family. And Kate herself was from St. Louis—not even from Louisiana.

So there was certainly some ambivalence. But as Emily Toth writes, Kate Chopin was also a bit of a show-off, or at least she presented herself that way, just because she was different. There are stories of her riding horseback in smart outfits and even smoking, doing things that were probably shocking to provincial people.

Do you think Kate Chopin was a feminist?

She probably would not have identified as a feminist. In fact, she apparently had opportunities to join the contemporary women's suffrage movement but didn't. However, you can't look at her fiction and not infer that she really thought women were getting a raw deal, and she didn't like it. Basically, I think Kate Chopin just wasn't an organization person. She wasn't a feminist in the sense of being an activist.

But if feminism is having a woman-centered perspective, absolutely yes. She clearly saw the inequities of women's lives, and she often chafed at some of the limits of being female in her own life, like not being encouraged to walk around the city by herself or being taken seriously as a writer. But she also deeply appreciated some aspects of being female, like the deep joys of maternity and sensual pleasures. Luckily for her, she apparently had an indulgent husband and enough money to avoid some of the most painful disadvantages of being a woman—though she did see them around her.

Were Chopin's writings impressionistic?

When one talks about her writing as impressionistic, that doesn't necessarily mean that she was directly influenced by Impressionist art. But Kate Chopin was very well informed about contemporary aesthetics, and what was happening in art, in literature, as well as in music, which emphasized the ways that the senses are more important than the idea. There were literary models for the kind of writing that she was doing—notably and specifically Guy de Maupassant, whom she credits with teaching her "how to see": how to convey reality through material impressions. So I wouldn't call Chopin "an Impressionist," but I would certainly call aspects of her writing impressionistic.

Chopin was so incredibly sensual. Do you think she had any inkling of how bad the reviews would be for The Awakening?

Not about *The Awakening*. I don't think she did. But she did when she wrote an even more sensual story, "The Storm" (after she had finished *The Awakening*, but before it appeared in print). She didn't even try to publish "The Storm." She kind of knew that she could go a little farther. She had the skills and the vision to do more than she had already done in *The Awakening*. But I also think that she believed that she had observed the boundaries in *The Awakening*, that she hadn't gone too far.

Remember, too, she was immersed in European literature, whose limits were much broader than those of American fiction. She probably figured that she was pushing the boundaries but that she hadn't actually crossed them. Maybe she hedged her bets, but she was wrong—wrong in an unexpected way. What the critics objected to, as you may recall, was not Edna's risqué behaviors but that Chopin didn't punish her for them. It wasn't the sensuality, which is quite subtle and which critics often admired, but it was the lack of moral retribution. Sin is fun to watch, but sinners should be punished!

Barbara, you were once a member of a religious order. This is interesting, since Kate Chopin's best friend became a nun. How do you feel Kate evolved either toward the Catholic Church or away from it?

I've always thought that Kate Chopin's Catholic upbringing was extremely important to her writing, as was her friendship with Kitty Garasché. But what I think Catholicism gave Chopin was its sacramental vision: that the Earth, the material universe, is sacred and offers a way—maybe the only way—into the transcendental.

I mean, Protestantism sort of says, "No, no, no. Materiality is dangerous. You have to go straight to the word." No pictures, no art, only the word—and music, which is itself relatively abstract. There is much truth and beauty to that approach. But Catholicism has always said, "Oh no, you need smells. You need bells. You need to affect all emotions and senses."

I think that's what you see in Kate Chopin's fiction. There's a little story called "A Morning Walk" that she wrote late in her career, about a man who is a bit of an agnostic, even an atheist. He happens to attend an Easter service, and while the service doesn't move him (actually, it bores him), the trees and the light through the windows, Nature, that's what gives him a profoundly religious experience. And I think that's the Catholicism or the effects of Catholicism as a way of thinking about the world that you see in Chopin.

Do you know what happened between Kitty and Kate at the end?

I think they had just gone their separate ways. After a visit with Kitty, Chopin wrote another little story, "Lilacs." What you can gather from that story is that religious life seemed to Chopin too confining, that it didn't allow for enough of the physical, the essential sensuality that humans need. I mean, that's the bottom line there. Religious life just wasn't Chopin's way. Of course, I could be projecting!

Chopin was buried in the Catholic church, though apparently, she didn't attend Catholic services in the latter part of her life. She was, as we say, a "fallen-away Catholic." She had a very good Catholic education, and I suspect her kids did as well. She was definitely culturally Catholic.

"Culturally Catholic": What does that mean?

Well, I guess I mean that it's also what you two are, because you lived in New Orleans for so long, right? You have a Catholic sensitivity. Maybe you went to Mass from time to time; you let your kids learn about the Pope in school; you weren't offended by taking off on Catholic holy days or Mardi Gras. You probably thought meatless Fridays and Lent and nuns in full habits were perfectly normal.

In Chopin's time, Catholicism in New Orleans would've been inescapable. And when she went up to Cloutierville, there probably were Protestant churches, but they were hardly significant.

Is there any topic about Chopin that you would love to see more writing about or research into?

Well, I would pose it this way: Is there anything more to be said about Shakespeare or Brontë or Woolf? Is there anything more to be said about Chopin? Of course, there's more.

Every generation will need to see for itself what Chopin offers us. Her stories remain very rich; even her poems might have some interest. I'm sure that there's even more that can be done with gender, race and class and how she dealt with those topics.

In her writings, Chopin doesn't go a lot into the backstory on people or into the political, social context. Her stories are very relational. Can you tell us more about her writing?

I think she was not unaware of what she was doing. Again, writing about Ibsen and Zola, she insists that what's important is not really the social context. That perspective is, by the way, why she probably wasn't an activist. But she was deeply interested in relationships, in how people deal with each other. Even so, social contexts, like the disadvantages of being a woman or being a married woman, were evident to her. To some extent, she could even see some of the handicaps of racism, though not nearly so clearly. What she saw around her, she inevitably incorporated in her fiction, but those issues were never her focus.

Is there anything else you'd like for readers to know about Kate?

I don't want readers to think that Chopin was so discouraged by the criticism of *The Awakening* that she quit writing. That wasn't true. Emily Toth has made that clear over and over. If you just look at Chopin's personal writings from that time: Was she disappointed? Was she heartbroken? Maybe. What writer likes a bad review? But most writers don't go out and commit suicide or quit writing. They just say: *Alright, I'm going to do that again.* The notion that Kate Chopin's fiction was banned, that she lost heart and quit writing is a real disservice to her, because she didn't. She kept writing. Her health failed about that time, and she wasn't able to write as much. But that's a very different story.

The other thing I'd like for people to appreciate is that she was very savvy about her market—her audiences. She wrote about what she knew and what she thought would sell. She didn't compromise herself, but she might have thought: *I'm going to write about what I want to write about, women and relationships and interesting social dilemmas, but I'm going to set things here in Louisiana, which everybody loves reading about since it's so different.* Look at her early work. She tried setting stories in Missouri, in historical contexts; she even set one story in Paris. They didn't sell. She started setting her stories in Louisiana. Bingo! Editors and audiences asked for more—and Kate Chopin obliged.

Interview with Dr. Bernard Koloski, Chopin Scholar

For over three decades, Dr. Bernard Koloski has studied Kate Chopin. He wrote *The Historian's Awakening: Reading Kate Chopin's Classic Novel as Social and Cultural Theory* (2018), *Awakenings: The Story of the Kate Chopin Revival* (2012) and *Kate Chopin: A Study of The Short Fiction* (1996). Dr. Koloski is a professor emeritus of English at Mansfield University in Pennsylvania.

Why do you think Kate Chopin wrote most extensively about Louisiana?

From 1870 to 1884, when she lived in Louisiana, Kate Chopin observed carefully the people in New Orleans and the rural areas of the state. Later, back in her hometown of St. Louis, now a single mother raising six children and looking for some extra income, she saw that magazine readers loved stories about the lives of people in different parts of the country—"local color," such stories were called. Chopin was a good storyteller, so she drew on what she knew from her life in Louisiana, and she sold her stories about Creoles, Acadians (Cajuns), Blacks, Native Americans, Latinos and others, including mixed-race people. *Vogue* bought and published nineteen of her stories. *The Atlantic* and other national magazines also published her works.

Why was Kate Chopin considered so risqué or taboo?

Kate Chopin published most of her short stories in the 1890s. So far as we can tell, publishers and readers liked her work and had no problems with it. But her 1899 novel, *The Awakening*, hit a raw nerve in the United States. We have no way to know what ordinary readers thought of it, but the newspaper and magazine critics who reviewed it were furious, calling it "unpleasant," "sordid," "unhealthy," "morbid," even "poison." Some of them understood that it was a beautifully written book, but their criticism of Edna Pontellier's adultery and suicide, what they saw as her selfishness, took hold, and the book was largely forgotten. It was the 1950s before people again began to read the novel for themselves. Two World Wars and the Great Depression had begun to change what people thought about Edna, and by the 1970s, when the new women's movement developed, a remarkable revival of Kate Chopin's writings was set in motion.

Why do you think The Awakening *is still popular today?*

The Awakening and a few of Kate Chopin's best-known short stories are about women seeking freedom, integrity and fulfillment. Chopin's fiction is popular today in the United States and abroad because of its intense focus on the inner lives of sensitive, intelligent, resourceful and often daring women who want to control their own destiny.

Was Kate a feminist (though the word wasn't used then)?

Today readers understand Kate Chopin as a feminist because of her stories about women wanting to live fulfilling lives. If feminism means writing stories like that, then yes, of course, Chopin is a feminist writer—and a very good one.

But readers today also understand—and dictionaries define—feminism in addition as "organized activity on behalf of women's rights and interests," as "advocacy of equality of the sexes and the establishment of the political, social, and economic rights of the female sex."

Kate Chopin did not write about such organized activity or advocacy. She was suspicious of writers who focus on contemporary social issues. In a published review, she complained about the Norwegian author Henrik Ibsen, whose plays (like *A Doll's House*) often deal with moral and ethical conflicts between individuals and the traditional societies they inhabit. Chopin did not like what Ibsen wrote. Kate argued that

> *human impulses do not change and can not so long as men and women continue to stand in the relation to one another which they have occupied since our knowledge of their existence began. It is why Æschylus is true, and Shakespeare is true to-day, and why Ibsen will not be true in some remote tomorrow, however forcible and representative he may be for the hour, because he takes for his themes from social problems which by their very nature are mutable. And social problems, social environments, local color and the rest of it are not of themselves motives to insure the survival of a writer who employs them.*[28]

It's helpful to keep in mind that Kate Chopin lived and wrote her stories before our grandparents were born. We ought to be careful attributing our twenty-first century sensibilities to her. We don't know if she would have been comfortable being thought of as a feminist as we today understand that word. She did not write to change the world. She wrote to describe accurately what she found in it.

But that need not affect the way we may want to use her descriptions as evidence of the need to improve the lives of women today.

What are key ideas that feminist theorists identify in the book?

I have shared a model of what feminist theorists seek to accomplish. In Kate Chopin's book, such theorists see correctly that in Louisiana in the second half of the nineteenth century, Edna Pontellier's life is severely limited, tightly controlled, by patriarchal rules and traditions growing out of Roman Catholicism combined with Victorian or Puritan practices. Her life is limited and controlled, too, by the American legal system, by the "separate spheres" logic in which men live in a public world while women live in a private one, by the absence of adequate education, career choices, economic resources, birth control, abortion, safe hospital childbirth, etc. And wealthy nineteenth-century American wives like Edna were pressured by a host of daily social demands, many explained in popular etiquette books that spelled out the duties expected of them. One such book has 352 pages of advice.

What is accurately depicted in **The Awakening***?*

Kate Chopin accurately shows us that the story told in the novel is set among Creoles: easygoing, urban, English- and French-speaking Roman Catholics. And she is accurate in showing us that Edna Pontellier, raised among stern, rural, Kentucky and Mississippi Presbyterians, is an outsider in that world. Edna is a wife and mother living in her husband's culture, struggling for autonomy in an environment that is strange and invigorating—and upsetting for her.

Chopin shows us that Edna's struggle is personal. She shows how Edna had a deeply troubled childhood after her mother died and is a private person. (Chopin's original title for the novel was *A Solitary Soul.*) But we also see that Edna's struggle is social, cultural and religious, defined by the conventions of wealthy people at the time and intensified by obligations imposed upon upper-class women. That struggle is set in motion by differences in ethnicity—by Edna's emotional interactions with several Catholic Creoles. And it results in what Chopin calls Edna's "despondency."

Is anything that Kate wrote about in **The Awakening** *still prevalent today?*

Probably most readers would say that much of Edna's social and cultural oppression continues today for many women whose lives are still controlled by patriarchal, religious and other attitudes.

What are your students' responses to The Awakening*? What are their questions/misunderstandings/critiques?*

I've taught Kate Chopin's novel and discussed it with students and colleagues here in the United States and in France, Poland, Russia, India and Kuwait. It's a great book to teach, because it's short and pretty clear—even for people who are not native speakers of English—and it brings up fascinating subjects to talk about in a classroom.

People everywhere, I've concluded, respond to stories in the context of their own lives and experiences. In the States today, some people understand Edna as admirable—daring in her attempts to break free from the social and cultural roles of her times. Some see Edna as irresponsible in abandoning her duties and her children and then having sex with another man and drowning herself because she refuses to live a life she cannot change. And some are torn between those two ways of understanding Edna. They find themselves confused, conflicted, frustrated—feeling upset by her actions yet sorry for her.

Outside the United States, in places where people have vastly different economic, cultural and religious backgrounds, Edna comes across in different ways. In the 1980s in Poland, when the country was still under Soviet-style communism and there were shortages of almost all consumer goods, an irritated young woman told me the trouble with Edna is that she doesn't need to stand in line to buy bread.

In general, many people living in the poorer places where I've worked did not have much sympathy for Edna. They saw her as simply rich and privileged, someone who does not have real problems and so has time to be thinking about what might be missing in her life. Others thought she is just having a midlife crisis. And still others saw her as complex and deeply troubled but also intelligent, sensitive and courageous.

What would you like readers to know about Kate Chopin?

I would like them to know that Kate Chopin's fiction is so widely read, so widely taught and so widely loved today because Chopin writes truthful, beautiful stories. Those two qualities—truth and beauty—go hand in hand. Chopin describes the truth about life as she has known it, and she describes it in beautiful prose, in smooth, clear, flowing language, often in lovely, powerful sentences that bounce around in people's minds decades after reading them:

Model of Feminist Theory

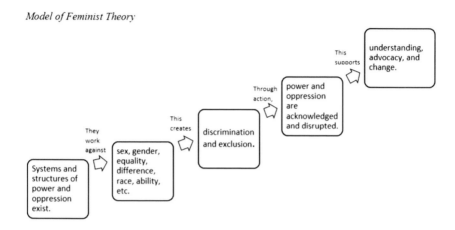

Models of Feminist Theory. *Courtesy of Dr. Bernard Koloski.*

> *Even as a child she had lived her own small life all within herself. At a very early period she had apprehended instinctively the dual life—that outward existence which conforms, the inward life which questions.*
> *She was becoming herself and daily casting aside that fictitious self which we assume like a garment with which to appear before the world.*
>
> *There would be no one to live for her during those coming years; she would live for herself. There would be no powerful will bending hers in that blind persistence with which men and women believe they have a right to impose a private will upon a fellow-creature.*
>
> *I would give up the unessential; I would give my money, I would give my life for my children; but I wouldn't give myself.*

Such sentences are hard to forget.

In the final analysis, once we have sorted through the basic facts of her life, what we have left of Kate Chopin is her fiction. That's all we know of her—and all we need to know.

INTERVIEW WITH DR. HEIDI PODLASLI-LABRENZ, INDEPENDENT CHOPIN SCHOLAR

Dr. Heidi Podlasli-Labrenz is an independent Chopin scholar residing in Germany. In 2016, she organized the first international Kate Chopin Symposium, called "More Than Just a Southern Writer," which explored Kate Chopin's German connections and took place in Knoop's Park in Bremen. She serves as the German bibliographer of the Kate Chopin International Society. In her book, *Inspiration and Transcendence* (Lexington Press, forthcoming), Dr. Podlasli-Labrenz investigates primarily the influence of the women writers of the German Vormärz on the work of Kate Chopin.

How were you first introduced to Kate Chopin?

It was a coincidence. I needed to draft a paper for my class on what I would be working on for my dissertation. I had some ideas in my head, and they wouldn't work out. So I went to the library at Ball State. And I was meandering through the aisles. Then, all of a sudden, this book found me: *The Awakening*. I just pulled it out, and it has never left me since. I was really stuck, I was at this dead-end street, and I needed to come up with the paper, and then I was reading the book and I just devoured it. I thought, *I always liked existentialism…*

Can you share with us more information about Kate Chopin's connections to German culture?

In her diary, Kate was writing about German women, who are so independent. She was taken aback by their autonomy and their deliberate behavior. I realized that she was really talking about German women who were living during the period of the first German Revolution, which was in 1848.

St. Louis was one of the cities of the German triangle, along with Milwaukee and Cincinnati. Those three cities were heavily populated with German immigrants.

I think Kate was very fascinated that people did not want to live under another reign of a German duke. When you talk about women like Kate walking alone—up until the German Revolution, German women were not allowed to walk alone freely. They always needed to be helped by a chaperone. That was something that changed.

What is your perspective of German women today? Do they still have that sense of autonomy or independence?

No, I think that German women have moved backward. The thing is that I only learned about the events that were leading up to the German Revolution of 1848 through my work on Kate Chopin. I think with everything going on in the twenty-first century, people have lost sight of the German Revolution.

German women during the revolution were much more emancipated, much more geared toward living independently, having their own income, having their own social and financial independence. Some of that has been lost.

What struck me is that Kate was really taken aback by the liberty that German women took to pursue their own lives. They went out and made their own decisions. I think that she really admired that.

There is this one entry in her European diary that says, "I was really struck with the relationship between a young lady and her maid." She said that they were not really acting as if they were a lady and a maid. It was this perspective on living in an egalitarian society, pushing toward democracy, which was essentially the purpose of the German Revolution.

Oscar Chopin's business dealings brought the couple to Germany on their honeymoon. Tell us more about what you learned about Kate's honeymoon in Germany.

There is one entry on July 8, 1870, where she said they arrived at the free city of Bremen, which is my hometown. She wrote, "In the afternoon, we took a wonderful ride into the countryside, and we met the richest man in Bremen. We had a wonderful afternoon there, we enjoyed German tea."

I thought, *One of these days, I'm going to find out why they were there and why they were able to have access to the richest man in Bremen.* Ludwig Knoop was the European cotton baron. He was so rich, his factories were in Estonia (which was part of Russia).

This park was a summer residence that he had designed for his retirement. And it was guarded. Everything was just done to make the visitors from the South comfortable. The reason why Oscar went there was he wanted to make connections. He wanted to have someone to buy the cotton that he was factoring.

Can you share with us more about your understanding of Kate's Creole connections?

The Creole connections have been an important part in Kate Chopin's life. This is where Adolph Frerichs (Ludwig Knoop's nephew) and Marie-Josephine d'Aquin (Adolph's Creole wife) come into play. You can read about these connections on the plate that has been placed in front of Frerichses' house in the Garden District (I was struck by how close it was to the last residence of the Chopins in New Orleans). I talked more about the Frerichses in my essay on the International Cotton Traders. Ursula von der Leyen, the current European commissioner, is Ludwig Knoop's great-granddaughter.

Are there any other German connections you're aware of in Kate's life?

Her mentor, Dr. Frederick Kolbenheyer, was Austrian and was inspired and influenced by the same ideas that Kate Chopin had. If you're looking at the German authors that she was reading, those all belong to the school of the German Romantics.

The school of the German Romantics influenced a movement that is known as the *Jungdeutschen* (Young Dutch). This was a group of philosophers, writers and thinkers who were all pushing for a unified Germany. At that point in time, the thirty-seven states were each ruled by one sovereign (Prussia and Bavaria were the most important ones). And they wanted to have a unified Germany.

Kate's mentor wanted to have the same thing but not for Germany, for Austria. I went to Vienna and did some research at the Imperial Library, and you can find quite a few things about Dr. Kolbenheyer. He was notoriously known for asking for the resignation of the emperor. And so, he was kindly invited to leave.

Then he went to St. Louis because it belonged to the German Triangle, which did not necessarily mean that they were all Germans, many were speaking German. I mean, the Austrians were speaking German; the Swiss were speaking German; there were parts of France where you were speaking German. So it's called the German element of Milwaukee or Cincinnati or St. Louis. They had their own German social clubs. They had their own festivities. Kate was entrenched in this German life.

The Awakening *is one of the most popular books in university syllabi. Why do you believe Kate Chopin's writing is still relevant today?*

She wanted to write for her own audience, but what she was writing, like with the story "An Egyptian Cigarette," it's true for eternity. These aspects of German women's independence, of claiming autonomy, of being autonomous human beings, not being reduced to some female who is inferior to someone. She was always claiming that a woman has the right to make her own choices in life.

Is there anything else you're curious about learning about Kate Chopin?

Well, I'm researching German influences in Katherine O'Flaherty's life. I'm curious if she absorbed any German influences when she was living in New Orleans. This is unknown.

New Orleans had a huge German population, even had a few German newspapers, when Kate lived there, like the *Daily German* newspaper. There was also the German National Theater [in the 1870s]. I'm pretty sure that she went there—the building is no longer there—but it was only a few steps from the Chopins' home on Magazine Street.

Chapter 4

HISTORIANS DISCUSS
NINETEENTH-CENTURY FASHION

INTERVIEW WITH HOPE HANAFIN,
COSTUME DESIGNER

Hope Hanafin has designed costumes for the theater, opera, ballet and for films, including *A Lesson Before Dying*. Previous vice-president of the Costume Designers Guild, she has been nominated for two Emmy awards for her costume designs.

Can you explain more about clothing in the 1870s–80s?

The first thing I would say, just to put things in perspective, is that people had so much fewer clothes. When you think of what an armoire is, that's what held your wardrobe. In fact, even the wealthiest young women in London and Paris, when they'd got married in their wedding dress, they would wear that for that next social season for all the events. They'd wear it to the opera; they'd wear it to a ball.

They would heavily invest in clothes, which were exponentially more expensive than ours today but not necessarily proportionally. You have what you wear in the morning; you have what you wear to receive guests; you have what you wear to visit people; you have what you would change for dinner, what you wear to a concert. So it really is specific to the time and the social occasion, as opposed to now, where the richest people in LA are going to dinner in a T-shirt and a baseball cap, and that's what they wore home from the gym. So it was very segmented.

Another thing to think about, when describing Kate Chopin and her day, is that she's wearing all natural fibers. Things get wrinkled, and there are creases and things were not laundered as often. A man's suit, for instance, would really only be brushed and maybe cleaned once a year. It's better for the clothes, but you'd brush the dirt off, not send them through an inorganic dry cleaner, which destroys the fabric. There was much more care to your garments because they had to last.

Having a dressmaker was very, very common. Also, having laundress was very, very common. And then you would have a seamstress, who would come in once or twice a year to do alterations and let the hems down on your children's clothes. You passed clothes down among your children. They had a deeper hem, so you could let them up and let them down.

What was the hardest thing about women's clothes?

Getting in and out of them.

Women's clothing restricts movement. I'm old enough to have worn a merry widow (a woman's undergarment combining a bra with a corset ending just below the waist and garters for stockings) once or twice in my life. It is restricted. The arm holes are high and tight, and it was done on purpose: so you didn't move.

Everything was made to keep you erect and your steps small. Think of it as when you see a woman in a kimono walk in those shoes and how upright and constrained she is: it's the same principle.

To be in society was really to be contained. Your voice is contained, your movements are contained, society is contained and your knowledge base was contained.

As you and Kate were both students of the Academy of the Sacred Heart, can you tell us more about this experience?

It's a pretty interesting order. It's a French order. When people say nuns here, they think it's like those Irish nuns, some of whom had an eighth-grade education. Mothers of the Sacred Heart were not that at all. They were all educated, and their mission, in part, was to educate elite young women so they would know how to be in society—meaning you only had to relate to one man in your life, your husband, but you had to know how to be in the company of other women. That was part of what the education was—and to do charity work. But they originally came to St. Louis to work with Native populations. They're all called Mother, not Sister, by the way. And by their last names.

Going to boarding school at age five was not that unusual. My grandmother did it. It wasn't like being sent away. Of course, my grandmother was with her sisters. I'm a fifth-generation Sacred Heart girl.

Gouter (*goûter* means "to taste" in French) were the treats that you would get after class. It means a snack or something like that. Cache cache (from *cacher*, French for "to hide") was a game we always played. And then primes (evaluations) were every Friday, where you all line up, there's a roll call—citing if each student was very good, good or less then good. Reverend Mother gives a little speech. Then you stand up class by class and curtsy…

My grandmother did tell me that you got dressed under your nightgown, so you'd put your nightgown on over your head and then you'd take your clothes off and you'd keep your nightgown on. Similarly, you got dressed under your nightgown and then you took your nightgown off. So you lived in a dorm, which was rows of beds, but you never saw each other naked.

What kinds of travel clothes would Kate have packed for her European honeymoon?

Well, you would have your trousseau, right? So everything would be new. That's a tradition that doesn't exist anymore, but a trousseau would be all new lingerie, all new nightgowns. And you'd say "wedding trip," not "honeymoon," to be proper.

Kate would always have her hat and gloves, her reticule or small purse, which would be leather in the daytime and beaded at night. She'd have walking shoes, which would be like a high button shoe, at night. It would be an evening slipper, which could be either calfskin or satin, depending on if it was for a ball or not. Calfskin you could get by with. Once again, you don't need that much. And they were moving, so she could wear the same dress to the opera in every city. They weren't staying with someone where they had to show off in that way.

Since it was the summer, she doesn't need an evening cape, though you usually did have a wrap. She'd probably have a short evening cape and two evening dresses. Travel ensemble would be the equivalent of a coat and skirt and blouse jacket.

You'd have an outfit for the train or boat. Maybe two of those, three at the most.

It would not be unusual for servants to only have one or two things. So having any more than that made you rich. At least when I was young, when a guy asked you out, you went out and bought something new. I went to an award ceremony, I worried, *What am I going to wear?* It just wasn't the same then; unless you were the empress of Austria-Hungary, you just wore your one party dress to every event.

Many report that women back then weren't allowed to walk outside alone, ever. And pregnant women weren't seen in public. What have you found?

Pregnant women did go out in public, but they just had to disguise themselves. Up until what, thirty years ago, maternity clothes were all about disguise, right? In the fifties, they were Peter Pan collars and little bows. It's like you weren't supposed to figure out how you got pregnant, so you made everything look really innocent and sweet.

I think at late-term pregnancy, people would stay home. Also, remember that giving birth was really dangerous.

Can you tell us more about pregnancy attire?

For the maternity corsets, there was a change in time where they're making them more of a basque shape, a straight up-and-down and not trying to nip in the waist—so they would have healthier babies and not be so constrained.

What sorts of undergarments did women wear back then?

When considering the undergarments, especially if you're doing anything in terms of intimacy, consider how long it takes to get there. I mean, having worked in New Orleans, wearing a corset in the summer just seems brutal to me. And the shoes, and the stockings, and the pantaloons, and the chemise, and then the corset over that and then the petticoat over that—it's layer

This rustproof corset (1898–1902), which is made of silk cotton, metal and potpourri, was featured in the *Fashioning America: Grit to Glamour* exhibition at the New Orleans Museum of Art. Corsets were adjustable to the wearer's body and became a key export for the United States. *Photograph by Rachelle O'Brien.*

upon layer upon layer, which is actually an interesting idea to think about what that means, that you never go out kind of undefended.

Kate had five sons and one daughter. And basically every eighteen months or so, she was having another baby. So she really wasn't out of maternity clothes.

Can you tell us a little bit about children's clothing?

Clothing is very age-specific. The younger boys wore more like a smock and shorts, to the knee. As you got older, it would become knee pants. And even older, it would become long pants with a jacket. The little boy's pants would be cotton; as you went up, it was wool. There was a long-sleeved white cotton shirt underneath that's more smock than we're used to.

Can you tell us about how location influenced fashion?

It'd be interesting; Kate Chopin wouldn't have afforded new clothes when they moved to the store in Cloutierville. She would've had more elegant clothes there, which might've set her apart. Or, she would've had to wear the simpler dresses, and hang the good stuff in the closet. It's just an interesting thing to think about that when she moved to Cloutierville.

Kate enjoyed horseback riding on the bayou. How would a woman get onto a horse in nineteenth-century clothing?

Well, there's a whole different riding outfit. The dresses in this period are not very full. You could have pants underneath them, and then a skirt over; that probably would make the most sense. And that would also help with chafing.

INTERVIEW WITH DR. LINDA WELTERS, FASHION HISTORIAN

Dr. Linda Welters teaches fashion history and material culture at the University of Rhode Island, where she also serves as the director of the graduate program and the Historic Textile and Costume Collection. Dr. Welter's publications include *A Fashion Reader* (2022), *Fashion History: A Global View* (2018), *Twentieth-Century American Fashion* (2005) and *Down by the Old Mill Stream: Quilts in Rhode Island* (2000). Dr. Welters has served as editor of *Dress*, the scholarly journal of the Costume Society of America.

What sorts of clothing or uniforms would Kate have worn?

Kate would not have worn a school uniform at the Academy of the Sacred Heart School; uniforms were not adopted in parochial and private schools in the United States until the early 1900s. Archival photographs of the academy reveal that students did not wear uniforms until the early twentieth century. Even sports teams at women's colleges, such as Wellesley College in Massachusetts, wore uniforms only after 1875.

I've done some research on the Litchfield Academy in Litchfield, Connecticut, one of the earliest girls' schools in the United States. In the

1820s and 1830s, their students were "expected to rise early, be dressed early, be dressed neatly, and to exercise before breakfast." Dressing "neatly" meant wearing styles appropriate to the fashions of the period.

While fashions for girls mimicked those of adult women, their youth was denoted by hem length and hairstyle. Young girls wore short dresses or skirt/blouse combinations with shortened hems until well into their teenage years. They wore stockings and ankle-high boots that buttoned at the sides or were pulled on the foot. The latter boots had elastic insets at the sides and were known as congress gaiters. These were popular when Kate was in school. Slip-on flats were worn, too. Underwear would have consisted of drawers, an undershirt, petticoats and, as a girl matured, a corset and corset cover.

Hairstyles were a second indicator of youth; girls wore their hair down and softly curled, often embellished with bows. When a young woman reached the age of sixteen or seventeen, she began wearing her hair up. Bonnets were worn outdoors. Coats and shawls kept girls warm in cool weather.

Quaker bonnet, (1850s). The Quakers (or Religious Society of Friends) dressed in plain and modest clothing as part of their spiritual practices. In the nineteenth century, Quakers were known for refusing to wear cotton that was produced by enslaved labor. This bonnet was exhibited in 2023 in *Fashioning America: Grit to Glamour* at the New Orleans Museum of Art. *Photograph by Rachelle O'Brien.*

In 1855, Kate would have worn above-ankle dresses with full skirts gathered at the waist. She would have worn petticoats to make the skirt stand away from the body. About that time, cage crinolines (steel hoops attached to tapes) were introduced, and she might have worn one of these in the later 1850s and 1860s. Children's versions exist in museum costume collections. A possible outfit for a girl in her teens in the 1860s might have been a Garibaldi blouse and skirt, or a Zouave jacket over a blouse and skirt.

What sorts of clothing would the nuns have worn?

Nuns' attire consisted of a habit specific to their religious order. Images of the sisters who taught at the Academy of the Sacred Heart show that they wore long black dresses gathered at the waist with high necklines and long sleeves. Headgear consisted of long black veils that reached below the knees. Their hair was covered in the front by black fabric and their faces framed by starched white fabric. This restrictive head covering originated as a medieval headdress known as a wimple. Most nuns' habits had ropelike belts hanging from the waist. The habit of the Sacred Heart order included a large cross suspended from a cord around the neck.

Archival photographs from St. Louis's Sacred Heart Academy are online, showing exactly what the nuns would have worn. The oldest one is probably from the early 1870s, judging by the fashionable ensembles of the young women, which was just after Kate left the school.

Catholic nuns continued to wear the same habits until the 1960s, when the Second Vatican Council liberalized Church doctrine. Many communities changed to modern clothing, creating dilemmas for women accustomed to wearing a habit every day. Of special concern was hairstyling.

As a debutante participating in balls and social parties in St. Louis, what sorts of fashion would Kate have worn?

Evening dresses differed from day dresses in the materials they were made of, as well as exposure of the neck and arms. Kate's evening gowns would have been made of silk fabrics, possibly trimmed in tulle. In the late 1860s, the bodices would have been cut low at the neck with short sleeves that started at the shoulder. Kate would have been tightly corseted. Skirts were still very full but had started shifting volume to the back with apron-like

This evening gown (1866–67), once owned by Madame Olympe Boisse, was exhibited in the *Fashioning America: Grit to Glamour* at the New Orleans Museum of Art. *Photograph by Rachelle O'Brien.*

draperies ending in bows or long tabs at the back waist. Evening dresses were not purchased ready-made. She might have patronized a dressmaker for this type of gown. Kate would have accessorized with jewelry, flowered headpieces, fans and gloves.

How might Kate have dressed during the 1870s in New Orleans, both inside of and outside of the home?

The bustle reigned in the 1870s and 1880s. This was a silhouette that consisted (in most cases) of a tight-fitting bodice and a separate skirt. The skirt had apron-like swags and draperies lifted up at the back with the assistance of a substructure called a bustle. The basic bustle silhouette went through several changes over the two decades. Kate would have kept up with the changes by making alterations to existing clothes or ordering new ensembles.

Kate would have worn a bodice (like a fitted jacket) with a bustled skirt during the day. One-piece princess-line dresses were an alternative toward the end of the 1870s. Since Kate was part of a prosperous family, she probably dressed more formally for dinner. Possibly she had a lady's maid to assist her in maintaining her wardrobe and dressing for various occasions.

Outside the house, she would have been expected to wear a bonnet with her ensemble. Fashion historians read of outfits appropriate for visiting, traveling and walking, although distinctions between them are sometimes hard to discern. Shawls had become outmoded with the ascent of the bustle; a short coat-like outer wrap called a dolman became popular, as it accommodated the bustle without crushing it. Gloves and a parasol completed the outfit.

How did pregnancy and postpartum phases of life during this decade affect Kate's choices of clothing?

When pregnant, and around the house in the morning, Kate probably wore a loose-fitting one-piece dress called a wrapper. Many of these exist in our collection at the University of Rhode Island, mostly of cotton but some of silk with velvet trim. Louisiana has a warm, humid climate, so probably wrappers in cotton fabrics would have been her choice. Cotton calicoes were widely popular during the entire time period during which Kate lived. White cotton fabrics may have been acceptable choices for wrappers in the South. Wrappers functioned as house dresses, so Kate might have worn these after pregnancy as well.

Kate might have patronized local dressmakers, but she also might have sewn some of her own things. The writer Emily Dickinson, from a socially prominent New England family, made some of her own clothes (see Daneen Wardrop, *Emily Dickinson and the Labor of Clothing*, 2009).

How did the mourning rituals affect Kate's clothing choices?

Mourning etiquette for a widow required wearing full mourning for a year and a day (e.g., black dress, bonnet, maybe mourning jewelry). Brooches, bracelets, rings and necklaces made of black jet became popular, as did jewelry made from the deceased's hair. Mourning crape (now spelled "crepe") was the preferred fabric, but dull black silk was also acceptable. After the first year elapsed, the widow wore half mourning until the end of the second year. The colors could be dark colors like gray or purple. Shorter periods of mourning were acceptable for other relatives.

In rural Louisiana, Kate enjoyed riding horses. What would she have worn?

Horseback riding required a riding habit. This was a fitted wool jacket and matching skirt that was longer on one side than the other to cover the legs when riding sidesaddle. If Kate departed from this protocol by riding bareback astride the horse, then she might have endured criticism. There was a miniature top hat that usually went with this outfit. Boots would have been standard, thus not out of the ordinary. Riding outfits were made by tailors rather than dressmakers.

What were rural folk wearing at this time in the South?

Louisiana is home to people who were forcibly removed from Canada during the eighteenth century. Known as Acadians, or Cajuns, they dressed in what could be termed ethnic styles. They wove their own fabrics for a long time after the Industrial Revolution. Other rural folk may have only minimally followed fashion.

How might have Kate's French fashions been different from local styles in rural Louisiana?

During the 1870s and 1880s, many wealthy American women ordered their clothes from Paris. Americans traveled to Europe via ship and shopped at London tailors and Paris couturiers and dressmakers. Charles Frederick Worth was the most famous French couturier, but there were others. Pingat, Félix, Laferriere and Roger were his competitors. Kate might have visited these couture designers and left her measurements; afterward, she could order new styles to be sent to her in America. Kate married on June 9, 1870, and honeymooned in Europe. By July of that year, France was embroiled in the Franco-Prussian War; Paris fell in January 1871. Thus, Kate would have had to shop and place her orders early in her trip before returning to the United States because of the impending war.

Wealthy women also patronized dressmakers, who closely followed the latest styles from France. Many ladies' magazines published fashion plates with detailed descriptions so that dressmakers and home sewers could copy them. Paper patterns, pattern drafting systems, sewing machines and other sewing aids were available by 1870, which would have made it easier for New Orleans dressmakers to create fashionable, well-made clothes.

How could different groups of people's clothing options have created friction between Kate and the locals?

Anyone who can afford nicer, more fashionable clothes than her peers might provoke jealousy. It was expensive to follow fashion and to have a complete wardrobe suitable for every occasion. Fashion changed rapidly, and not everyone could follow each dictum from the ladies' magazines. Another consideration is that Kate might have been exposed to the practices advocated by dress reformers, who prescribed less restrictive styles. The few photographs of Kate available online indicate that this was not the case, since she appears fashionably dressed in every image.

Kate is said to have loved the color lavender. What is the history of lavender in fashion?

The preference for lavender after the mid-1850s is well-documented. Prior to 1856, all dyestuffs came from natural materials such as plants, animals and minerals. Purple was a difficult color to attain up to this point in time. Purple came from the glands of mollusks and enjoyed rarity value in the ancient world; the phrases "royal purple" and "born to the purple" attest to its status. The color became wildly popular in the later 1850s and 1860s, even into the 1870s, for dresses and accessories. Empress Eugénie of France wore purple; so did Mary Todd Lincoln. Thus Kate was in good company in her affection for lavender. It also implies that Kate followed fashion closely.

Chapter 5

NEW ORLEANIANS CONVERSE ABOUT KATE CHOPIN FILMS

Interview with Dr. Barbara Ewell
and Rachel Grissom

Cofounders of Ripe Figs Productions, Dr. Ewell and Rachel Grissom created three short films inspired by the works of Kate Chopin: *Ripe Figs*, *Dr. Chevalier's Lie* and *Regret*. They collaborated with Artemis Preeshl, Loyola University theater professor. Their short films have attained global acclaim: *Ripe Figs* won Best Short Film at the Raleigh Film & Art Festival and *Dr. Chevalier's Lie* was nominated for Best Director at the Southern States Film Festival.

Can you tell us more about your short films inspired by Kate Chopin?

Barbara Ewell: Artemis Preeshl, a colleague at Loyola University, approached me with her friend and associate, Rachel Grissom, to ask about making films together, based on Kate Chopin's short stories. They knew how to make films, but they wanted me to be the Chopin expert—the dramaturge.

I'm quite proud of our films. They really are adaptations and interpretations of Chopin's original tales; they are not literal in any sense.

But Rachel and Artemis had some interesting angles on the issues those stories embody, and I loved working with them. After doing the usual film festival circuit, we eventually found a permanent home for the films on the Kate Chopin International Society website.

Can you describe some of the issues in the films?

BARBARA EWELL: In two of the films, race was the issue. We began working on them right before the beginning of Black Lives Matter. *Ripe Figs* replaces Chopin's White characters with Black ones, a historically feasible option, since there was a prominent class of wealthy Black Americans in Louisiana in that era. The story and film explore issues of aging and youth and the way those two don't always communicate. A young woman wants to be free, and an older woman can't really let go of her goddaughter.

While Chopin's very short story "Dr. Chevalier's Lie" was about class and social prejudice, we added racial prejudice, even as we highlighted the misunderstandings and even violence that many women face.

Finally, while Chopin's story "Regret" implies lesbian relationships, our version puts that issue front and center. Our film examines homophobia in a contemporary context and shows how hard it is for a gay couple to live in a small Louisiana town.

Actually, in her story, Chopin also meditates on maternity. Her unmarried character, Mamzelle, has never missed having a husband. But then one day, her neighbor drops off her kids for her to take care of. At first, she doesn't know what to do with them. But by the time they leave two weeks later, she realizes that *that's* what she has missed: children, motherhood. She didn't need a husband, but she has really missed the kind of sensual intimacy that motherhood offers. We try to show that, as well.

Why do you think Kate Chopin's writings have relevance today?

RACHEL GRISSOM: Like a lot of women even now, she started analyzing life and trying to figure out how our lives are constructed, and how society constrains us. She was writing about race, class and gender. And she was absolutely writing about what she knew of female presentation, what was acceptable and what brought happiness.

What was your vision behind what you wanted the films to look like?

RACHEL GRISSOM: "A Respectable Woman" for us was a natural place to start because it was one of the more easily accessible pieces that she had written for a modern reader. It was about the constraints of domesticity, female sexuality, class.

"Dr. Chevalier's Lie" is very much about the social consequences of female agency in female sexuality. It was influenced by the literal story that the character (a prostitute) killed herself one night in the French Quarter. Dr. Chevalier goes to see the body and declare her death. It's very routine for him. Later, he makes the funeral arrangements for her in New Orleans. This proper burial inspired immediate social acceptance of the woman, something she had never received. We were literally making a story about who has the authority to the truth, who gets to tell the official story of a woman's death.

This is what makes Kate Chopin relevant to modern audiences: Chopin would not have participated in or even understood the concept of a political movement, like Black Lives Matter or Say Her Name, but she was writing about the power that authority has over truth and justice, and who matters.

Opposite: Kate Chopin's grandson David Chopin and his wife on their wedding day. *Photograph provided by Kate Chopin's great-granddaughter Annette Chopin Lare.*

Chapter 6

HEIRS PONDER LEGACIES

INTERVIEWS WITH GREAT-GRANDCHILDREN OF KATE CHOPIN: ANNETTE CHOPIN LARE, SUSIE CHOPIN, GERRI CHOPIN WENDEL AND TOM CONWAY

We were grateful to complete several interviews with the grandchildren of Kate Chopin's son George "Doc" Chopin (1874–1952).

HERITAGE

How have you learned about Kate Chopin?

SUSIE CHOPIN: We learned about Kate's life mostly through those who wrote about her, and we remain grateful to them all. A lot wasn't said in the family about Kate and her works—not because they weren't proud of her. My dad said that Doc and his siblings were very proud of her. I think it was maybe a combination of her profession/success/criticism, which was obviously unusual at the time for a woman. And, at the same time, I think it just wasn't the center of their own lives. Dad said that all Doc ever said about Kate was that she was a great lady.

We heard about her life in New Orleans and Cloutierville, riding bareback and smoking cigarettes. All the things a lady didn't do. I see her as a free spirit constrained in her times but staying true to herself.

Annette Chopin Lare: The family readily admits that almost everything we know came from the scholars. We feel really fortunate as a family. How many families have these scholars do this extensive research on their families and dig up all these records and all these wonderful old photographs? I'm kind of in awe of Emily Toth. She went to France to see where Oscar's father brought his family during the Civil War to keep Oscar out of the war. I just cannot believe the amount of research that goes into a biography.

What have you learned about Kate Chopin?

Tom Conway: Kate Chopin died in 1904, but it wasn't until the 1960s that she was rediscovered and became famous. In the early sixties, Per Seyersted, a Harvard graduate student and a Norwegian, wrote about her for his dissertation. He and Emily Toth and other academic researchers have since added an enormous amount to our knowledge of Kate and our family. Growing up in the 1950s, I remember that there was some divided opinion about Kate's writing and her life choices, particularly among my many Chopin and Gleeson aunts. But I think most of them admired her for her courage, even if they disagreed with some of her views.

Then in the 1960s, after Per Seyersted's work, there was the feminist movement in America, in my opinion, that made Kate famous. It is good that she finally got the literary recognition that she deserves. In addition to her "ahead of her time" feminist point-of-view of her main novel, *The Awakening*, she was an extremely good writer, and a good stylist. I have her short stories in a couple of locations—print and eBook. I read them all the time, even if I'm waiting in a doctor's office or on a plane or wherever; they're wonderful stories.

Annette Chopin Lare: Kate still shows up everywhere. When my sisters and I were on a road trip this year to the Women's Rights National Historic Park in Seneca Falls, New York, the gift shop was selling a book called *Short Story Masterpieces by American Women Writers*, which included "Desirée's Baby." And recently, a friend just sent me a photo of a plaque of Kate Chopin, which made her stop as she walked in New York City, not far from

Grand Central Station. I also just bought a new book of her short stories in French. And my nephew picked up *The Awakening* in Portuguese on a recent trip to Lisbon.

Did you learn about family connections in France?

ANNETTE CHOPIN LARE: I have connected with very distant cousins in France. We started corresponding, and we met them in New York City. In 2016, my husband and I also visited them in Paris and in the south of France. We went to the Champagne region, not far from where Oscar went to school. One of the French cousins had traced the family back about four hundred years to a tiny village called Lagery. This was one of the more memorable days of my life.

Oscar Chopin's father was the one who came over from France and settled in Louisiana. Oscar wrote letters to his relative in St. Louis, a banker named Louis Benoist (his home is actually a place you can visit, a wedding venue called Oakland. I've been there). Oscar also wrote to his uncles and cousins in St. Louis and in France. In one letter, Oscar was talking about—in today's terminology—basically how the St. Louis women were "babes" and so much better than the Louisiana ones. All of this is written in French in this exquisite nineteenth-century penmanship. Somebody in France saved all those letters. Somebody went to the trouble of typing out all those letters [later]. These cousins that I reconnected with photocopied almost all this stuff and sent it to me. It's really fascinating because some of these letters go really far back—like the 1840s.

St. Louis

Share with us more about Kate's hometown?

SUSIE CHOPIN: People come to St. Louis, blink, and they're gone. If you give yourself a little time, you'll discover our many gems. We don't have a bustling downtown as some cities have. We're spread out in many suburbs, and it's a great place to live and raise kids with our beautiful riverfront, parks, the Arch, the Cardinals. And yes, it's also where Kate grew up. The home in the city where she was born is no longer standing, but her last home, where she died, still is in the Central West End on McPherson Avenue.

Kate Chopin's last house, St. Louis, Missouri. *Photograph courtesy of Susie Chopin.*

TOM CONWAY: There is an area in St. Louis known as the Central West End (CWE). Kate's last home was there on McPherson Avenue. T.S. Eliot, Tennessee Williams and William S. Burroughs (and other writers and artists) all lived in the CWE at some point in their lives, and now there are four individual busts of them, outdoors, on the four corners of the intersection of McPherson and Euclid Avenues. Appropriately, a very popular bookstore, Left Bank Books, is also on one of the four corners.

Tell us more about what you learned of Kate's Catholicism.

GERRI CHOPIN WENDEL: Kate's children were definitely raised Catholic. They all received the sacraments. In my family now, of the eight children, two are still Catholic. My kids were raised Catholic. And they have all baptized their kids in the Catholic faith. Certainly, Kate wrote about women being trapped in the expectations back then, but she still was living at a time where she had to follow what was expected.

ANNETTE CHOPIN LARE: My Dad said that his mother said that Kate Chopin read herself out of the Catholic Church. Kate was a member of a Catholic family, but she had given up her faith and had left the church. There was a lot of disapproval about—even the thought of—leaving the Church. There was this idea that if women got too many ideas that it would lead them to leave the church.

What did you learn about Kate's value of the social register?

ANNETTE CHOPIN LARE: Kate Chopin really wanted her daughter to have her "coming out," a debut. My mother told a story that Kate Chopin—and this may be an anecdote—but that it was very important to her that her descendants remained "society people." My parents were almost the opposite to society or country club people, but they and their siblings were in the social register. My mom did say that was because of Kate Chopin. Kate had made some kind of arrangement. She wanted her descendants to stay in the social register.

Describe Kate's gravesite.

ANNETTE CHOPIN LARE: Kate was able to be buried in Calvary Cemetery, which is a Catholic cemetery. I did hear this story that shortly before she died, supposedly someone had seen her on the steps of St. Francis Xavier Church, which is the church connected to St. Louis University. And from this, they surmised that Kate must have gone to confession and thus was welcomed back into the church and was able to be buried in Calvary Cemetery. Kate is buried with the Chopin family almost all the names around her grave are Chopin. Most of my aunts and uncles are there; my parents are there; a first cousin and her husband are there. Kate Chopin's grave is pretty plain. There's an epitaph with her name and the dates of her life, which were wrong. They have it down that she was born in 1851, and she wasn't. She was born in 1850. I believe Oscar is buried somewhere in the O'Flaherty plot nearby. I don't know why Kate wouldn't have been buried in the O'Flaherty plot, but she was buried with the Chopins. I recall my mother lay in bed and worried about poor Oscar being up there in an unmarked grave. At some point, she and my dad made a decision that they were going to have Oscar's name carved onto the back of Kate Chopin's gravestone.

Oscar Chopin's tombstone, Calvary Cemetery, St. Louis, Missouri. *Photograph by Susie Chopin.*

SUSIE CHOPIN: Years ago, I met a woman at the Missouri Historical Society who was doing her thesis on Kate. It was such a random encounter, because I just happened to be there, and she was leaving the next day. I'm not sure what those odds are that we even met. But I asked her if she wanted to meet my parents (since Dad is Kate's grandson) and if she wanted to go to Kate's grave. We drove up to the cemetery, and it was so humbling because she was standing on Kate's grave and she said, "She's right here. She's right here." It was very emotional for her, as well as for me.

LOUISIANA

What do you make of Kate's life in New Orleans? Her connection with Edgar Degas?

GERRI CHOPIN WENDEL: [When I teach about Kate Chopin's life,] the students especially love the Degas stories. I talk about Degas telling Kate about Berthe Morisot, the French Impressionist artist, and her sister, Edma. Edma married a man whose last name was Pontillon. Then fast forward a couple decades. When Kate needs a name for the protagonist in *The Awakening*, she uses Edna Pontillier. I love the Degas connection with Kate and the friendship they developed. Another connection to *The Awakening* involved Degas's brother, René, who had an affair with someone whose husband's name was Léonce. So when Kate needed someone who was a good provider but not necessarily a passionate partner, this name Léonce came back in *The Awakening*.

TOM CONWAY: For years, when I'd looked at the famous *The Cotton Office* painting by Degas, I'd always thought the stout man on the far right, looking through some ledgers, might have been Oscar Chopin. But the man in the painting has been identified as someone else. But it was fun to think it might have been Oscar. He was in the same business as the Musson and the Degas family.

There was also a similarity between Oscar Chopin's and Edgar Degas's relatives: their families yanked them out of New Orleans and got them to Paris during the American Civil War. I'm sure Kate and Edgar did meet in New Orleans. People would like to think they had an affair. But there's no evidence of that. I think it was and remains just gossip.

ANNETTE CHOPIN LARE: I am aware of Edgar Degas's stay in New Orleans while the Chopins lived there and the possibility that he gave Kate the idea, and even the names, for the main theme and characters in *The Awakening*. As an art history major, this is one of my favorite tidbits about Kate Chopin!

At one point, I heard that Kate's son Oscar was a cartoonist and that he was conceived when Edgar Degas was visiting New Orleans. And the idea went out like: Degas is an artist. Oscar became an artist. Kate and Edgar were there together in New Orleans. It's just this throwing out of these kinds of tidbits that really lack evidence. By all accounts, Kate and Oscar had a good marriage. He was much more tolerant of the kinds of freedom that she wanted.

Tell us about Kate's house in Cloutierville.

ANNETTE CHOPIN LARE: One summer, we drove south to New Orleans. We stopped in Cloutierville, and we were able to see the house where Oscar and Kate lived. It was a big house with a huge veranda. It burned down. I'm so glad we got to see it before that house burned. After living in cities her whole life—St. Louis and New Orleans—I can imagine Kate going absolutely crazy in this rural, provincial environment. Even when we were there, there was not so much as an intersection in Cloutierville, or at least where the Chopins lived; it was just a bend in the road. I was anxious to

Drawing of the Kate Chopin house. *Library of Congress.*

visit the local cemetery on our way out of town and see even older relatives, but there was a heavy storm, so we skipped this.

Do you think the burning down of the house was a mysterious fire?

ANNETTE CHOPIN LARE: I have never heard of anything about the cause of that fire. When we were there, it was the Bayou Folk Museum. We met the curator and an English professor from Texas who just happened to be there. The bottom level was more like a barn, and the family lived in these four large rooms on the second floor, which was really common in the South. I think they were along a river, near the Red River. Oscar references the river in one of his letters.

What do you make of romantic speculations that people have made about Kate Chopin with Albert Sampitié?

ANNETTE CHOPIN LARE: There was this speculation that Kate Chopin might have had a romance with Albert Sampitié in Louisiana. The idea would be thrown out in one book, and then in the next book, it was presented as fact. Whether or not this occurred when she was still married to Oscar, I don't know. I was kind of like: Where's the evidence? I think a lot of this speculation was anecdotal, being handed down through small-town gossip. My mother grew up in Mississippi, and she said: "If your evidence is small-town gossip, you've got nothing."

SUSIE CHOPIN: A number of years ago, a researcher came to our house to interview Mom and Dad. My mother, who wasn't related to Kate by blood, was her biggest defender. She was always happy to talk to anyone about Kate. I remember the researcher kept picking at the affair question. She wanted it validated. But there was no validation, and there was no way to find proof. Whether Kate did or didn't have an affair with Albert—to me, is neither here nor there. It was her life. But that always bothered my mom. She also agreed that if it was true then it was true, but with no proof, it wasn't nice to force it. We take some things with a grain of salt because no one knows for sure.

TOM CONWAY: There were strong rumors that Kate had had an affair with Albert. But again, I don't think there's any really firm evidence. There was clearly some resentment toward her by local people. Some people thought that Kate looked down on them as "just country folks." She was from New Orleans and from St. Louis, and she had traveled in Europe.

KATE'S WRITINGS

What was your first introduction to the writing of Kate Chopin?

GERRI CHOPIN WENDEL: My real first introduction to Kate was in college, when I took a Women in Literature class. I was not an English major, but I had to take one more class to graduate. I opened the catalog that we had to open to pick our classes, closed my eyes and hit Women in Literature. I signed up for the class not having any idea what was being taught. It was all short stories and one novel, *The Awakening*. I'm looking at the syllabus, thinking, "Oh my gosh, this teacher is going to think I know all this stuff about Kate Chopin." And so, when the teacher, a doctoral student, took roll, she got down to my name and froze and said, "Chopin." And she looked up: "No?" I said: "Yeah."

How did you relate to Kate's writing then and now?

GERRI CHOPIN WENDEL: Back then, I was within six months of graduating, getting married to the love of my life, and I couldn't wait to have children. I could not identify with Edna. But fast forward ten years. I have three children. I'm in a mom's club, with an informal book club. I said, "Let's read *The Awakening.*" I read it, and it was a whole different experience. I'm an exhausted mother with three children and my identity is my kids—and so I got Edna. It was such a stark reality. The words hadn't changed, but my perspective had changed from being a blissful, soon-to-be married lady to an exhausted mom of three.

Do you have any short stories by Chopin that are your favorite?

TOM CONWAY: There are two that are famous and have surprise endings. One is "Desirée's Baby." The other is "The Story of an Hour." But I like a lot of the other ones, too, such as "A No-Account Creole." I pick them at random from the table of contents and read and reread them. But those two stick in my mind. They're clever and well written. The pacing is good. The characters are believable.

Early on, some critics dismissed Kate as "just a local colorist," but anyone who has read her carefully, in my opinion, can see her understanding of human nature and the wider, permanent relevance of her work. Sometimes, she'll get a little carried away in her writing, but every writer does. I certainly do.

Her novel *The Awakening* is very good. I've read it four times. It's been read in high schools and universities for decades. I love her powers of description and her psychological insights. She was fluent in written and spoken French, and I think she was influenced by at least three well-known French writers: Flaubert, de Maupassant and George Sand. (George Sand had had a relationship with Frederic Chopin. As far as I know, he was not related to Kate Chopin.)

You can see in Kate a very sophisticated mind that has been developed early by the love of the women who raised her after her father died and developed further by the affection and discipline of the Sacred Heart nuns, who educated her.

When did you realize that Kate Chopin had international significance?

GERRI CHOPIN WENDEL: We were living in London one semester, and my daughter was in the British schools. She was in the equivalent of our junior high. She came home from school one day and said, "Mom, we're going to read 'The Story of an Hour' in our English class." That's the first time it hit me—the international impact of Chopin. When I came back from London, I actually started doing my own research and giving the high school talks, probably fifteen years ago.

Do you think Kate was a feminist—though the word wasn't used then?

SUSIE CHOPIN: As far as her writing, I remember doing an interview, and the interviewer commented on Kate being a feminist and ahead of her time, as most people believe. I do understand that thinking, but I said that I didn't look at her the same way. She didn't write about any subject that wasn't a part of society one hundred years before her time, nor one hundred years after her time. She wrote stories that were lovely and visual but also touched on everyday topics such as biracial relationships, infidelity, even drugs. These topics weren't new. Kate wrote stories about what she observed in her life and yes, imagined. I don't think she was making an incredible feminist statement nor ahead of her time. In her works, I don't call her a feminist. I call her courageous in the time she lived in for walking into publishing companies (and self-publishing) and successfully, as a woman, giving the world her art.

As far as the person, Kate seems to me a combination of a very socially conscious woman who grew up privileged and understood society's boundaries, yet at the same time, I picture her a free spirit who bucked the social conventions when it was in her nature to do so because I do believe she loved herself. And if that's one definition of feminism, then yes, she was.

GERRI CHOPIN WENDEL: Kate just wrote stories about what she observed in her life. I don't think she was making this incredible feminist statement. She wrote about reality.

LEGACY

What's been your experience seeing Kate's writings at the Missouri Historical Society?

SUSIE CHOPIN: It's very emotional when I go to the historical society. The first time I actually saw her handwriting was very special for me—even seeing her signature. Articles of hers, like clothes, her personal possessions, other writings, old manuscripts—they've got to be in someone's attics, but much we've never seen. So, when I saw her handwriting, it was something I had of hers. And I should say it's not because she was a "famous" writer. It's because it was my great-grandmother's handwriting.

ANNETTE CHOPIN LARE: The Missouri Historical Society has most of Kate's items. I remember visiting the Missouri Historical Society in St. Louis. When we told them who we were, they generously brought out all the original Kate Chopin photos and artifacts they had and let us handle them. I suspect that her daughter probably picked up most of her personal items. She and her daughter were quite close.

Can you tell us more about your experiences teaching Kate Chopin to high school students?

GERRI CHOPIN WENDEL: I put Kate's family tree on the board when I teach. And when you see it, there are just hundreds of descendants because there were all these big families who just kept having kids. As I tell them about Kate's life, I put a red *X* through the name when she loses someone—either in death or in her friendship.

It gets to the point where the students react with, "Not another one." Kate Chopin buried so many people in her life. That is perhaps the most impactful thing that the students see. These are young people who maybe haven't experienced much death at all. The impact of Kate remaining who she was in the midst of so much loss in her life is a powerful message.

One student wrote, "I've been in a dark place like Kate was, and I know I can keep going." One girl drew a bird, of course referencing Kate's wings. Then another young lady drew a grand piano with a music sheet on it that was Chopin. How awesome for that particular student to make this connection to the composer and Kate? I talk a lot about the love of music that Kate had and the power of music and *The Awakening*. As teachers, you never know what your students are going to take in or pick up.

When I talk to the students about *The Awakening*, I say, "Who were Edna's two love interests?" It was Ro*bert* Lebrun (you had the "Bert") and the *Al*cée Arobin (the "Al"). And Kate's love interest in Cloutierville was Albert Sampitié. When I take that name and divide it, they go: "Oh my gosh." I love being able to give them that connection to her life. That's what has been so thrilling. Another group of female high school students really felt sorry for Robert in *The Awakening*, and they had T-shirts made and wore the T-shirts to class. It had a picture of Robert Lebrun on it and said, "#Robert." The three classes signed the back of it because they really developed this love and sadness for Robert. They think he really loved Edna but he was not able to have her in his life.

INSPIRATION

Did Kate's life inspire or influence you?

TOM CONWAY: I always admired her writing style, but I also admired her because she had to deal with a difficult life. It wasn't a terrible life, but it was very difficult at times, and she had to work her way out of Oscar's debts after he died, pull herself together and support her children by her writing. I would love to have known her and talked with her about her life, her views of society, our family and her writing. She had to have been a fascinating person.

SUSIE CHOPIN: Her being inspires me. She had a varied life of privilege and of loss. She lived in a socially bound world, yet loved herself enough to be herself. She picked herself up after her husband died and found a way to keep going with six kids. Truly inspiring. As far as her writings, I'm more of a historical fiction reader, so I've never really been inspired in that sense. Not that her subjects aren't interesting, and I've read all of her works. But as an adult, I would never have picked up her works because I don't think they would have appealed to me. I remember reading *The Awakening* at age twelve, and it read more like a Harlequin romance. Again, I'm more into history. But I reread *The Awakening* again as an adult, while going through a difficult time in my life. I strongly related to Edna this time around. And I remember saying to myself, "How did Kate know I needed to read this right now? How did she know that I would relate to Edna and that she would give me strength?" I'll always be grateful to Kate for that, and I thanked her for looking over me. I'm a big believer that our ancestors are all around us. That was the moment her writing inspired me.

We all feel very, very blessed to have Kate in our lives. Thank you, Rory and Rosary, for helping share my beloved great-grandmother with the world.

Interview with Jeff Glenny, Descendant of Edgar Degas

Can you share with us family stories about Edgar Degas?[29]

My family would point out our great-grandfather (René Degas) and great-uncle (Achilles De Gas) and great-great grandfather (Michel Musson) in the *Cotton Office* painting. And Mother would talk about Degas bronzes at her grandfather's house on Second Street and how he'd tap his pipe into the horse sculptures by Degas.

What have you learned about your relative who was René Degas's granddaughter?

Dora Odile Musson (Degas) was very handy. Mother said they were raised in genteel poverty. They were very productive due to the Depression, even made their own beer. During the Depression, the family lost a fortune, like many others. They grew up on Saratoga Street, off Carrolton Avenue. There was a break-in at our family's house on Saratoga Street, and items were stolen. The robbers likely knew what they were going in the house for. Some Degas original artworks were there.

Edgar Degas's maternal family members were buried in St. Louis Cemetery No. 1 in New Orleans. Oscar Chopin's parents were also buried in the same cemetery. *Photograph provided by Jeff Glenny, great-grandnephew of Edgar Degas.*

Did your great-grandfather have any connections to the Cotton Exchange, where Oscar Chopin and René Degas frequented?

My great-grandfather Edmund Jefferson Glenny I was my namesake, and he was the president of the New Orleans Cotton Exchange (the centralized forum for the trade of cotton, established in 1871).

Have you visited the Degas family tombs in New Orleans?

My cousin Terry Martin and I visited our Degas ancestor graves in St. Louis No. 1. I have a New Orleans Diocese pass to visit the tomb. I had to prove my family lineage to get the pass. Michel Musson and his daughters are in the same crypt. The Rillieux crypt is facing the sun, with names inscribed in marble. Everything is written in French.

Chapter 7

MORE DISCOVERIES ABOUT KATE

Interview with Sister Margaret Munch, RSCJ, Academy of the Sacred Heart

Kate Chopin was raised Catholic and enjoyed her time as a student at the Academy of the Sacred Heart (1855–69). We were grateful to connect with Sister Munch, a Sacred Heart nun in Missouri, to learn more about Sacred Heart traditions.

Sister Margaret shared more about the founder of the Society of the Sacred Heart, St. Madeleine Sophie Barat (born in 1779):

> Sophie considered the service of education as the primary means by which the Society would carry on its mission of communicating the love of the Heart of Jesus. For her, education was never the end. The end was to rebuild the fractured world around her in hope; the means was forming young people to intelligent faith, compassionate action, and courageous hope (Sacred Heart Educators: An Orientation to Mission).

What is education like at Sacred Heart schools in Missouri?

Love has always been integral to life in Sacred Heart schools. The students have to know that they are loved and have entered into a family. This leads to self-confidence.

"Happy and blessed by God is the large family of the Sacred Heart." This family spirit continues today. In fact, students from the 1800s would feel right at home in any current Sacred Heart school because St. Madeleine Sophie's vision continues to the present.

Was there a rule of silence in the schools?

Yes, there was such a rule. It led to an atmosphere that was conducive to study and thought, as it minimized distractions. It's not quite as quiet these days, but students did travel in silence from room to room. Apparently, there was a time and place for conversation!

EXPLORING THE ARCHIVES AT THE ACADEMY OF THE SACRED HEART

Theresa Grass, archivist at Sacred Heart Academy in St. Charles, Missouri, and Michael Pera, archivist in St. Louis, shared photos of Kate O'Flaherty, Kitty Garesché and Lily Garesché (1866), as well as the earliest photograph

Academy of the Sacred Heart students. The earliest photograph in the academy's records of City House students, circa 1880. *Provided by the Academy of Sacred Heart, St. Louis, Missouri.*

of City House circa 1880. They also provided us information about Kate's entry as a day pupil in 1857 and her time as a boarding student for a few months in 1855.

THE ART OF THE DIARY

Kate Chopin's first biographer, Daniel Rankin, studied Kate Chopin's Louisiana diaries and interviewed her associates and their descendants. In this section, we share excerpts about Kate's life in Louisiana from his 1932 biography, *Kate Chopin and Her Creole Stories* (University of Pennsylvania Press).

Kate Explores New Orleans

Kate Chopin must have traversed the routes of the entire street railway system of New Orleans in the grotesque little cars of that period. The passenger on entering dropped the fare in a box. Meanwhile the driver—totally unconcerned about the riders within his jolting car—seated on a stool behind a dashboard reinforced with a stout facing of sheet iron, managed the mule as best he could. Car bells jingled to the regular or irregular ring of the animal's hoofs upon the cobble stones.

In these "sight-seeing" notes, Kate Chopin gives no indications of her own opinions, no expression of her reflections on places visited or people encountered.

Frequent mention of the New Orleans levee indicates her interest in the scenes along the river front—the diagonally wedged-in boats, the stevedores, the piles of cotton and other merchandise....Unconventionality never bothered her.[30]

A New Orleanian Friend's Reflection on Kate and Oscar

According to Rankin, Mrs. L. Tyler was a friend who visited Oscar and Kate's home in 1878 and 1879. She described her friends:

Oscar, ever jovial and cheerful and fun-loving and really very stout, liked to romp with the children through the house and about the gardens. "I like disorder when it is clean" was his favorite saying. Kate was devoted to Oscar and thought him perfect. She enjoyed smoking cigarettes, but if friends who did not approve of smoking came to visit her, she would never offend them. She was individual in the style of her clothes as in everything else. She loved music and dancing, and the children were always allowed to enjoy themselves. The long summer vacation times were spent with the children at Grand Isle.[31]

Chapter 8

REMEMBER ME

A Timeline of Kate Chopin and Louisiana

1805

Thomas O'Flaherty, Kate Chopin's father, is born in Galway, Ireland.

1818

January 13: Victor Jean Baptiste Chopin, Oscar Chopin's father, is born in Picardie, France.

1825

Marie Julia Benoist, Oscar Chopin's mother, is born in Louisiana.

1828

July 11: Irene Eliza Faris, Kate Chopin's mother, is born in Missouri.

1844

SEPTEMBER 30: Aurelian Roselius Oscar Chopin is born in Louisiana.

1850

FEBRUARY 8: Katherine O'Flaherty is born in St. Louis, Missouri.

1855

NOVEMBER 1: Thomas O'Flaherty Sr. dies in the Gasconade Bridge Collapse in St. Louis, Missouri.

1869–70

Katherine O'Flaherty debuts in St. Louis, Missouri. She likely meets Oscar Chopin at the Oakland house, which is owned by Louis Benoist (Oscar's uncle).

Kate Chopin writes the short story "Emancipation. A Life Fable."

1870

APRIL 13: Marie Julia Benoist dies in Louisiana.

JUNE 9: Kate O'Flaherty marries Oscar Chopin in St. Louis, Missouri.

JUNE–SEPTEMBER: Kate and Oscar travel to Europe for their honeymoon.

OCTOBER: Pregnant Kate (age twenty) arrives in New Orleans. She and Oscar move into a home in a charming residential section at 443 Magazine Street.

NOVEMBER 18: Victor Jean-Baptiste Chopin dies.

1871

Oscar sets up his cotton factoring business in a little office on Union Street (No. 26) in New Orleans.

MAY 22: Kate gives birth (age twenty-one) to her first child. Her son, Jean-Baptiste, is born in New Orleans.

1872

OCTOBER: Edgar Degas, French artist, lands in New Orleans. He resides with his brother (René Degas), uncle (Michel Musson) and their children in their rental home on Esplanade Avenue.

FALL: Both John McEnery (Democrat) and William Kellogg (Republican) claim victory in the contested 1872 Louisiana governor's election. Some extremists lead a coup, but Kellogg remains in power during the remaining years of the Reconstruction, 1873–77.

1873

Oscar moves his cotton merchant offices to an elite address at 65 Carondelet Street in New Orleans.

MARCH 5: During the First Battle of the Cabildo, members of the White League try to seize the police station at Jackson Square.

MARCH: Edgar Degas suddenly departs New Orleans and returns to France, with over twenty paintings he created in Louisiana.

SEPTEMBER 24: Kate gives birth (age twenty-three) to her second child. Her son, Oscar, is born in St. Louis.

DECEMBER 27: Kate's brother, Tom Jr., is killed in a buggy accident in St. Louis, Missouri.

1874

SPRING: Oscar and Kate attend the opening of the Eads Bridge across the Mississippi River in St. Louis.

LATE SUMMER: Oscar and Kate move to Constantinople Street, on the northeast corner of Pitt Street in New Orleans.

SEPTEMBER: In the Battle at Liberty Place, 8,400 White Leaguers attack the Metropolitan Police in New Orleans.

OCTOBER 28: Kate gives birth (age twenty-four) to her third child. Her son, George, is born in St. Louis.

1876

JANUARY 26: Kate gives birth (age twenty-five) to her fourth child. Her son, Frederick, is born in New Orleans.

Oscar and Kate move to bigger house on 209 Louisiana Avenue (now 1413) between Coliseum and Prytania Streets, around the time of Frederick's birth. This rental house is in the Garden District, and the property had extensive gardens.

1878

JANUARY 8: Kate gives birth (age twenty-six) to her fifth child. Her son, Felix, is born in New Orleans.

Oscar moves his business to have more extensive office space. His new office is at 77 Carondelet Street. Oscar's cotton brokerage faces challenging times due to a small cotton yield loss. Oscar offers extravagant advances to planters.

JANUARY 16: Oscar's brother, Lamy Chopin, marries his second wife, Miss Cora Henry, daughter of the Hon. Joseph Henry.

1879

Oscar's business goes bankrupt. He settles his debts and moves the family to rural Louisiana. He invests his remaining money in a general store in Cloutierville.

DECEMBER 31: Kate gives birth (age twenty-nine) to her sixth child. Her daughter, Lélia, is born in Cloutierville, Louisiana.

1882

DECEMBER 10: Oscar (age thirty-eight) dies from malaria; Kate becomes a widow (age thirty-two).

1882–84

Kate manages the general store and Cloutierville property. These years are the probable dates of her romantic attachment to Albert Sampitié.

1884

Kate leaves Cloutierville and moves with her children to her mother's home at 1122 St. Ange Avenue, St. Louis.
A collection of short stories by Kate Chopin, *Bayou Folk*, is published by Houghton Mifflin Company.

1884–1900

Kate visits Cloutierville frequently and stays with her Chopin relatives.

1885

JUNE 28: Eliza Faris O'Flaherty dies in St. Louis, Missouri.

1889

Kate Chopin writes short stories: "With the Violin," "Wiser Than a God," "A Point at Issue" and "Miss Witherwell's Mistake."
APRIL 26: Kate Chopin moves Oscar's body from Cloutierville to St. Louis. She buries Oscar in Calvary Cemetery in the O'Flaherty family plot.

1891

Kate Chopin writes short stories: "A No-Account Creole," "For Marse Chouchoute," "A Shameful Affair," "Dr. Chevalier's Lie," "Boulôt and Boulotte," "Love on the Bon-Dieu," "Beyond the Bayou," "After the Winter," "An Embarrassing Position," "A Very Fine Fiddle," "A Harbinger," "A Rude Awakening," "A Wizard from Gettysburg," "The Maid of Saint Phillippe," "The Going Away of Liza" and "Mrs. Mobry's Reason."

1892

Chopin writes "Ripe Figs," "The Lillies," "Loka," "At the Acadian Ball," "Ma'ame Pélagie," "Désirée's Baby," "The Return of Alcibiade," "Caline," "A Visit to Avoyelles," "Miss McEnders," "A Little Free-Mulatto," "Croque-Mitaine," "Old Aunt Peggy," "A Turkey Hunt" and "The Bênitous' Slave."

1893

Chopin writes short stories: "In and Out of Old Natchitoches," "A Matter of Prejudice," "Azélie," "A Lady of Bayou St. John," "La Belle Zoraïde," "A Gentleman of Bayou Têche," "In Sabine," "At Chênière Caminada," "An Idle Fellow," "Madame Célestin's Divorce" and "Mamouche."

1894

Chopin writes short stories: "A Respectable Woman," "A Dresden Lady in Dixie," "The Story of an Hour," "Cavanelle," "Juanita," "Regret," "The Kiss," "Ozème's Holiday," "A Sentimental Soul," "Her Letters," "The Night Came Slowly" and "Tante Cat'rinette."

1895

Kate Chopin writes short stories: "Odalie Misses Mass," "Athénaïse," "Two Summers and Two Souls," "Fedora," "Two Portaits," "Dead Men's Shoes," "Vagabonds," "The Unexpected" and "Polydore."

1896

Chopin writes short stories: "A Night in Acadie," "A Pair of Silk Stockings," "A Mental Suggestion," "A Vocation and a Voice," "Ti Frère," "The Blind Man," "Aunt Lympy's Interference," "Nég Créol," "The Recovery" and "Madame Martel's Christmas Eve."

1897

A collection of short stories by Kate Chopin, *A Night in Acadie*, is published by Way & Williams.
Chopin writes short stories: "Suzette," "An Egyptian Cigarette," "A Family Affair," "A Morning Walk" and "The Locket."
Chopin begins writing her novel *The Awakening*.

1898

Kate Chopin writes short stories: "The Storm," "A Horse Story" and "Elizabeth Stock's One Story."

1899

Chopin writes short stories: "Ti Démon," "A Reflection," "A Little Country Girl" and "The Godmother."
APRIL 22: *The Awakening* is published by Herbert S. Stone & Company.

1900

Chopin writes short stories: "The White Eagle," "Charlie," "The Gentleman from New Orleans" and "A December Day in Dixie."

1901

Kate Chopin writes short stories: "The Wood-Choppers" and "Her First Party."

1902

Kate Chopin writes the short story "Polly."

1903

Kate Chopin writes the short story "The Impossible Miss Meadows."

1904

August 22: Kate Chopin dies from a brain hemorrhage in St. Louis, Missouri.

Chapter 9

GOODBYE, KATE. LIVE ON!

With difficulty, we must say goodbye to Kate Chopin.

Still, so many questions linger. If Kate Chopin journaled her whole life, beginning at age ten, how and why did her Louisiana diaries disappear? Why didn't she try to write and publish in Natchitoches, Louisiana? (Maybe it's an absurd question, like: Why didn't Kate pursue opera singing while living in the swamp?) When her house, which was commemorated as the Bayou Folk Museum, burned to the ground, was it really an accident? Or was the fire foul play?

In Louisiana, Kate was an alien trying to meld in, which she mostly did. A keen observer going unnoticed. You can see more if you say less. She needed to show her smartness but not too much. Be seen but not shine too bright—people (still) don't enjoy that. But Kate was quietly judging, breaking down, holding up a man with broken dreams. And all the while, researching silently in Louisiana.

Maybe she loved the freedom of a Creole lifestyle in New Orleans. She could still read novels and newspapers there and dress exquisitely. Later, in the country, her outfits seemed outlandish, but could she afford to have new ones made? Or find anything to read? Boredom encouraged eccentricity. She must have been keeping up with speaking French to be able to translate Maupassant after all. Maybe Kate was intoxicated by love and excitement in New Orleans and the surprises of an insular world on the bayou. Maybe she was pushing down the pain of so many deaths in Missouri (her brothers, sisters, father and grandmother) by having so many births in Louisiana.

Did Kate know she'd outlive her Creole husband and leave Louisiana? Discarded, abandoned, afraid or free?

Kate harnessed her rich, tragic, exhilarating and terrifying experiences in New Orleans and rural Louisiana into short stories, plays, novels and poetry. We, your New Orleans authors, thank you for your life, your writing, your truth.

We bid you adieu, dear Katherine O'Flaherty Chopin. And with pride, we honor you as a daughter of Louisiana.

Goodbye, Kate. Live on!

ACKNOWLEDGEMENTS

Thanks to all the people who helped us get in step behind Kate Chopin and rallied us to say, "Yes, we can write her story. Yes, we can!" And thanks to God, who, in his mercy, makes us all able to soar.

No book comes to press without the riches and goodwill of many people neutralizing all the little and big problems that appear and disappear along the path. Like Hansel and Gretel, we mother and daughter team took hands and went down the road to what we hoped would be a book with a deep understanding of Kate Chopin in Louisiana. Many people helped us be fearless and not fearful, as we put one word after another. They made us grateful for what we had already done, while we pursued our goal to do even more.

Hail to our brilliant editor at The History Press, Joe Gartrell, who encouraged us. We wrote levitating on the cloud of hope that you created for us. And when our hearts hung low, you strengthened our resolve to keep moving forward, Joe. A thoughtful word, an enthusiastic email: all did not go unnoticed. Our happiness was doubled by the support of your team at Arcadia Publishing and The History Press: Jonny Foster, Erin Rovin and Hampton Ryan. Friends, you made us feel so appreciated, like we were being supported by guardians of American history. Well, it is The History Press, and our mission is to celebrate Louisiana's heroes.

We are grateful to the leading Chopin scholars for clarifying Kate's past, saluting her today and creating a vision for her future. Your genius sparked our research, but your presence was the strongest gift of all. Every minute we experienced with you was full of excitement, grace and knowledge:

Dr. Barbara Ewell, Dr. C.W. Cannon, Dr. Bernard Koloski, Dr. Tom Bonner, Dr. Justin Nystrom and Dr. Heidi Podlasli-Labrenz. Our thanks to additional colleagues who supported our research: Dr. Linda Welters, Hope Hanafin and Rachel Grissom. Much appreciation to the Missouri Historical Society for your steadfast preservation of Kate Chopin's papers.

We bow with gratitude to scholar and premier Chopin researcher Dr. Emily Toth, who paved the way for our study of Kate. Our hearts are conscious of the great treasure of your brilliant scholarship. Additional Chopin scholars and biographers, we remain grateful to you: Per Seyersted and Daniel Rankin.

Lest we take for granted the artists who deserve our gratitude, allow us to name them and salute them. We could not have created the complex picture of Kate's life in Louisiana were it not for their artworks. They noticed every detail in the Chopin sky, opening our eyes to even more of her world than we knew: Rachelle O'Brien, Robert Schaefer Jr., Cheryl Gerber, Billy Harris, and Insiah Zaidi.

All writers need noble souls guiding them who give them knowledge and hope. Mentors, we salute you: Mark Duplass and Eduardo Machado. You made us believe we could have everything in this world and that it was not unreasonable to expect it, if we worked from passion for excellence.

In this task of forging forward, agents and producers are the arbiters of hope. While we squirreled away hermetically writing, they trumpeted out our song. God be praised for their fearlessness: literary agent Linda Langdon and theater agent Tonda Marton and her colleague in Paris, Dominique Christophe. Deep appreciation to our film producer at MediaFusion Productions, Carole Bidault de L'Isle, and our brilliant colleague, Bill Goodman.

Our happiness was doubled by wonder at the support of so many. Thanks we give now for invitations to television, podcasts and programs: Peggy Laborde of *Steppin' Out* (PBS), Susan Larson and *The Reading Life* (NPR), WLOX Biloxi. Special thanks to journalist Alan Smason, who has long supported our projects.

Associates saluted us and introduced us to advocates, who would champion our work. Dear friends, we thank you: Anne Pincus, Nell Nolan Young, Carole DiTosti, Bryan Batt, Bob Browne, Megan Meehan.

Descendants of Kate Chopin, thanks for sharing with us the beauty of Kate Chopin and her family. You opened our eyes to a multitude of details that surrounded her writing. We hope we've done you proud: Annette Chopin Lare, Gerri Chopin Wendell, Susie Chopin and Tom Conway

(USA) and Florence Chopin (France). We grieve for the things we may have missed about Kate and celebrate the things we found.

Art historians at the Musée D'Orsay and the Louvre in Paris, you soared as a powerful catalyst for new discoveries of Edgar Degas, Berthe Morisot and Edma Morisot Pontillon. Every step forward with you lovers of the beautiful and the sensitive, we savored something bigger and better. For that we applaud you: Dr. Caroline Corbeau-Parsons, Dr. Isolde Pludermacher, Fanny Matz, Isabelle Gaetan, Fabrice Golec and Helena Mendes.

Global friends, you helped us grow and expand our knowledge of Kate Chopin and brought joy and laughter into our lives and into the lives of many who believed in the project: Nora Hickey M'Sichili (director of the Irish Cultural Center in Paris), Niall Burgess (ambassador of Ireland to France), Michèle Puyserver (France–Louisiane Association), Rodolphe Sambou (Consulate General of France in Louisiana) and Jacques Baran (cultural attaché of France to New Orleans), Solène Le Gallou (Foyer International d'Accueil de Paris) and the American Association of Women in Paris. We adore inspiring creatives in Paris, Normandy and Orléans: Genevieve Acker, Sylvie and Christian Raby, Annick Foucrier, Christel Coulon, Jean Pierre Bernard, Florie DuFour.

Our heart is full of the love treasure that Ireland has been to us and Louisiana: Dr. Eimear O'Connor (Tyrone Guthrie Centre) and our friends at the Irish Cultural Center in Paris: Loretto Mara, Donal O'Neill and Eugene Brennan.

Our knowledge of Kate as a girl kept expanding as historians helped us savor more details of her life. Brave and kind supporters of our Chopin research, we acknowledge you: Sister Margaret Munch, RSCJ; Theresa Grass; and Michael Pera. We share are deep gratitude to Degas's descendants and relatives, Jeff Glenny and Norbert Soulié.

So many colleagues made our fears vanish in the telling of the Louisiana story: Jackie DeBlieux (New Orleans Museum of Art), Rexanne and David Becnel, Patrick Ashton (Ashton's Bed and Breakfast in New Orleans).

Stacey Pfingsten (executive director, the Pitot House), the Orléans Club, the New Orleans Historic Collection, Janet Shea (Jefferson Performing Arts Society), the Missouri Historical Society and Café Degas. Special thanks to Joann Tournillon for her support in bringing the squad from Delimon to our signings and championing us with Entre Nous: Cecilia Victorian, Martha Priska, Margaret Shirer, Joy Cressend, we thank you.

Dear friends, you fueled our passion as we wrote about Kate Chopin in New Orleans: Jennifer Weidinger and Carl Rydquist, Dawn and Tanya

Henry, Lauryn Bymers, Dr. Katie Keresit, Georgie Simon, Cheryl Downey, Ann Jarrell, Brownie Fitzpatrick, David Holcomb, D.C. Larue, Mary Koppel, Billie Roe, Julie McKee, Lydia Ozenberger, Susan Izatt, Conner Kilian, Tracy Keenan, Heather Harper Cazayoux, Ray Fitz, Nikki Holley, Jeff Louviere, Vanessa Brown, David Hurland, David Schulingcamp, David and Debbie Temple, Rachel Friend, Maria Soccor, Anne Burr, Laurie Sapakoff and Evan Cohen, Voodou priestess Sally Ann Glassman, George Trahanis, Jim Bosjolie, Meghann Powers, Dennis G. Assaf, Loren Paul Caplin, Allen Hubby, Larry Harbison and Karen Engleman.

University of Southern California colleagues, you filled our hearts with Trojan courage: Dr. Melinda Thomas, Monica Keyes, Will Terry, Dr. Jennifer Hawe, Jessica Golden, Liz Phillips and Dr. John Keim.

A mother-daughter team, we completed this book venture buttressed by our family's love: our husbands, Bob Harzinski and Dr. Dasan Schmitt; our poet son/brother, Barret O'Brien; our daughters/sisters, Dr. Dale Ellen O'Neill and Rachelle O'Brien; our grandchildren/children, Olivia and Rowan. Arizona family, thank you for your joy, especially during Sunday's family home evenings: Victoria and Brett Schmitt, Jasmine Stevenson and Maya Schmitt. Louisiana family, thank you for always welcoming us home: Stephen and Pat Hartel, and Joe and Jean Hartel. Big hugs to our cousin Jay Nix and his Parkway Bakery and our cousins Eileen and Dale Nix, who celebrate all good creative things New Orleans.

Thank you to the Motherland, New Orleans.

We salute you, Kate Chopin.

And the most glorious, thanks to God and His angels of mercy, who keep us artists poised to imagine and to create.

With love from New Orleans, Louisiana,
Scottsdale, Arizona, and Paris, France,
Rosary O'Neill, PhD and Rory O'Neill Schmitt, PhD

NOTES

Part I

1. To learn more about Kate Chopin's personal diaries, refer to *Kate Chopin's Private Papers*, edited by Emily Toth and Per Seyersted.
2. Throughout this text, we reference research by Chopin scholars: Dr. Tom Bonner, Dr. Barbara Ewell, Dr. Bernard Koloski, Dr. Daniel Rankin and Dr. Emily Toth. For additional information about Kate Chopin, refer to the work of leading Chopin scholar Dr. Emily Toth. Her biographies include *Kate Chopin* and *Unveiling Kate Chopin*. Additional biographical information and archival materials can be found at the Missouri Historical Society.
3. For information about health and diseases in the nineteenth century, refer to the National Institute of Health and the Centers for Disease Control. Nineteenth-century illnesses included malaria, yellow fever, cholera and smallpox.

   Most people inflicted with malaria experienced bouts of chills and fever. Malaria patients could have recurring infections for two or three years and then be fine. The first pharmaceutical used to treat malaria was quinine (*Mayo Clinic Family Health Book*). In 1897, Sir Ronald Ross, a medical doctor, made the discovery that mosquitos transmitted malaria.

   Yellow fever began with jaundice, progressed to black vomit and ended in death with blood shooting out of the eyes, nose and ears.

   According to Bradshaw (2022), between 1863 and 1882, smallpox killed about 6,500 New Orleans residents. The smallpox virus caused a rash that started in the mouth, then morphed into open sores all over the body, which—if you survived—left scars. One-third of those who contracted smallpox died.

According to Steckel (1988), census data showed that of 329 children reported at less than one year old in 1850, about 23.4 percent failed to survive to 1860.

4. For more information about nineteenth-century female societal expectations, refer to the 1860 *Lady's Book of Etiquette*: "A lady was never supposed to go out without gloves.…A lady was supposed to change her pair of gloves several times a day, to protect her delicate hands.…The fit, design, and material all indicative of her class. A wealthy woman had staff to do labor of any kind, so fine gloves protected her delicate hands, and let everyone know so." Before the Civil War, a space called a "Ladies Ordinary" was set aside for women to protect them from dubious characters (*Women and Restaurants in the Nineteenth-Century United States*). See also: Moore's "Declared Insane for Speaking Up" and Pouba and Tianen's *Lunacy in the Nineteenth Century: Women's Admission to Asylums in USA*.

5. Many New Orleanians confronted racism. Local writers advocated for equality: "American journalist and novelist George Washington Cable fought against white supremacy and advocated for racial equality.…Alfred Mercier, a white Creole author who wrote in French, fell prey to 'lost cause' sentimentalism after the Civil War, though he continued to deplore race prejudice as a corrosive social force." See Schmitt and O'Neill's *Edgar Degas in New Orleans* (2023).

6. "Degas Is Here!" is a song performed by Blood Lovely (2023), with lyrics by Rachelle O'Brien.

7. For additional information about Degas's 1872–73 visit in New Orleans, refer to Schmitt and O'Neill's *Edgar Degas in New Orleans*. See also Edgar's letters in Feigenbaum's exhibition catalog *Degas in New Orleans: A French Impressionist in America*. Not all of Edgar's letters home to France from New Orleans survived, though over thirty have been preserved. There are gaps of time with no letters—either lost, stolen or burned. Rene Degas's belongings were burned when he abandoned his wife and children and left New Orleans with his mistress (who was also their neighbor).

8. Though the French opera was not in season when Degas visited, operas were performed before and after, while Kate resided in New Orleans: scores by Thomas (*Mignon* in 1871) and Bizet (*Carmen* in 1879); Beethoven's *Fidelio* (1870), *Der Fliegende Holländer*, *Lohengrin* and *Tannhäuser* (1877); Boito's *Mefistofele* (1881). See Belsom's research published with the *New*

Orleans Opera. Chopin was highly influenced by Wagner, who is directly referenced in *The Awakening* when Mademoiselle Reisz plays for Edna *Isolde*'s song, which is the aria at the end of Wagner's great opera.

9. Oscar Chopin and Edgar Degas's uncle (Michel Musson) and brothers (René and Achille de Gas) belonged to the Cotton Exchange. The Cotton Exchange building in which Oscar Chopin did business still stands in New Orleans. The Factors Buildings include a row of six four-story masonry commercial buildings, with examples of cast-iron decoration (designed in 1858). According to Rankin: "Business as a cotton factor was 'something tangible and intelligent' and profitable, for in 1873 Oscar added to his successful factorage business the more varied advantages of a commission merchant, and moved his office to elite Carondelet St." For more information about nineteenth-century cotton factoring, see *King Cotton* by Beck.

10. Refer to Nystrom's *New Orleans After the Civil War* and *Redeemer's Carnival: The Urban Drama of Reconstruction in New Orleans*. Fred Ogden led extremist forays to protect the 1872 election and led the militia mob's attack on the Cabildo. Nystrom describes masculine insecurities that drove many men's choice to engage in political violence. According to Taylor in *Louisiana Reconstructed*, "The election of 1872 was so shot through with fraud that no one ever had any idea of who actually won." See also "The Battle of Liberty Place," on the Law Library of Louisiana website.

11. Cloutierville was a small French village, located twenty miles south of Natchitoches on the Cane River. This town is one of the oldest European settlements in present-day Louisiana, a homeland of many multiracial Louisiana Creole people. According to Rankin, the house that Oscar and Kate moved into was a dwelling constructed in a style architects speak of today as the Louisiana type. Oscar's siblings resided nearby: Lamy had a big estate in Natchitoches and Eugenie had one in Derry.

12. Refer to Daniel Rankin, *Kate Chopin and Her Creole Stories.*

13. Additional information pertinent to Kate's connection with Albert Sampitié can be found in the research of Dr. Emily Toth. When Kate Chopin arrived in Cloutierville, Albert had been married eleven years. In 1891, Albert's legal separation from his wife was finalized. According to local legends, Kate flirted with townspeople, including the married roué Albert. Some scholars even say Albert Sampitié inspired her strongest male characters. But we suspect Albert never read Kate's work, or if he did so, he was amused or even flattered by it. Albert had limited education.

14. According to Rankin (1932), "To the town folks, as an elderly Creole lady in Cloutierville told me, 'her tight-fitting clothes, her chic hats and a good deal of lavender colors in all her costumes were constant sources of surprise. Her love of horseback riding they never understood,' the same informant declares, and adds, 'Her favorite costume was a fantastic affair—a close-fitting riding habit of blue cloth, the train fastened up at the side to disclose an embroidered skirt, and the little feet encased in pretty boots with high heels. A jaunty little jockey hat and feather, and buff gloves rendered her charming" (*Kate Chopin and Her Creole Stories*, 103).
15. Obituary of Oscar Chopin in an unidentified 1882 newspaper, via the Missouri Historical Society.
16. Refer to Kate Chopin's short story "The Storm."
17. Ibid.
18. This quote is cited in *Kate Chopin* by Dr. Ewell. Additional research into Kate and Albert's relationship can be found in Dr. Emily Toth's *Unveiling Kate Chopin* and *Kate Chopin*.
19. This was Maria Normand, daughter of Dr. and Mrs. Scruggs. In Chopin's stories, the characters mirror reality: Alcée sounded a lot like Albert, and the Acadian woman (Calixta) resembled Maria.
20. Toth identified the parallel of Edna Pontillier and Edma Pontillon in *Unveiling Kate Chopin*. She discussed the evidence that Kate Chopin and Edgar Degas met in New Orleans. We completed additional research on artists, Degas and Morisot, on-site at the Musee d'Orsay. Special thanks to Dr. Caroline Corbeau-Parsons, pastels curator, who provided Rory access for a close viewing of Berthe Morisot's undisplayed portrait of her pregnant sister. In it, Edma is dressed in black, but she wasn't necessarily in mourning. (Black was in fashion in Paris at the time of this intense portrait. Following the Franco-Prussian War, the virility of France was in question. French men were emasculated following their country's defeat; it was a time of wounded pride.) For additional information about nineteenth-century women artists, refer to publications by Barnes Foundation, Louvre Museum and the Metropolitan Museum of Art. Challenges faced by nineteenth-century women artists included being barred from exploring public spaces and not being allowed to travel unescorted. Bashkirtseff wrote: "What I long for is the freedom of going about alone, of coming and going, of sitting in the seats of the Tuileries, and especially in the Luxembourg, of stopping and looking at the artistic shops, of entering churches and museums, of walking about the old streets at night: That's what I long for; and that's the freedom without which one cannot become a real artist."

21. As cited by Nicole Myers, Metropolitan Museum of Art, in her article "Women Artists in Nineteenth-Century France."
22. From *The Awakening*.
23. See *The Awakening*.
24. To view the dates that Kate Chopin's short stories were written and published, refer to the Kate Chopin International Society: https://www.katechopin.org/kate-chopins-short-stories-composition-publication-dates/.
25. Excerpt from a *St. Louis Dispatch* article (January 16, 1898) in which Chopin answers the question, "Is Love Divine?"
26. From *The Awakening*.
27. Refer to *The Awakening*.

Part II

28. Quoted in Per Seyersted's *Kate Chopin: A Critical Biography* (1969), 86–87.
29. Jeff Glenny is the great-great-grandnephew of Edgar Degas.
30. Refer to Rankin's *Kate Chopin and Her Creole Stories*.
31. Ibid., 89–90.